"The church must change. The days of war between the saints must cease. If we are to fulfill the calling given to us to be *'a radiant church, without stain or wrinkle or any other blemish,'* we must learn how to recognize, discern, and defeat the spirit of Cain that exists to destroy the establishment of God's kingdom on earth. I stand in awe of Andrew Billings' courage, honesty, and prophetic insight to tackle such a poignant topic. With the utmost integrity as both a writer and a spiritual leader, Andrew unfolds revelatory truths that contain the power to liberate those who will read and set them totally free from the death grip of *the spirit of Cain*. This book is needed in this hour. A timely read that could set the church back on course."

—Joshua Mills
Best-selling author of *31 Days to a Miracle Mindset*
London, Ontario, Canada / Palm Springs, California
www.joshuamills.com

"My friend Andrew Billings is a faithful husband, a loving father, and a man of God whose humility shines through his writing. In his new book *The Spirit of Cain* he sheds much-needed light on how to be free from jealousy, envy, competition, and more. I know many will be blessed by this resource! Get your copy today!"

—Rick Pino
Heart of David Worship Center
Austin, Texas

"Every good gift and perfect gift is given by the Lord. I believe *The Spirit of Cain* is a revelation to all of us to examine ourselves in this area of competition and envy. Pastor Andrew Billings is a man of God, one of the Lord's warriors, a great husband, father, pastor, and leader. He is a prophetic voice to this generation, bringing much needed truths. I highly recommend his new book to you."

—Dr. Mary K. Baxter
Divine Revelation Ministries

"I have been friends with Pastor Andrew Billings for over a decade, and in this time I have seen Andrew demonstrate godly character, integrity, and honesty within our friendship. I heartily recommend not only Andrew's new book to you, but also Andrew's ministry. You will certainly be blessed by both as I have been. Andrew is a faithful husband and father and is a loyal friend. Andrew carries a message for our time that will not only challenge, but also help to reshape lives through simple, biblical truths that have often been overlooked."

—Pastor Andrew Robertson
The Dwelling Place
Auckland, New Zealand

"Having witnessed firsthand jealousy, envy, and unhealthy competition in the church and within humanity with catastrophic consequences, this book is eagerly awaited! *The Spirit of Cain* provides answers to many questions with powerful redemptive insights, that if received will be transformative, bringing healing, freedom, and unity in meaningful relationships.

Andrew Billings' faith and courage, perseverance, endurance, and yielded obedience from a heart of love and truth have positioned him to receive these revelations from the Lord, and it is for such a time as this that they available now through his book, for the body of Christ, and all who have a heart for a better world."

—Dr. Deborah Proverbs (MBChB)
Mental Health Medical Practitioner, New Zealand

"My good friend Pastor Andrew Billings is a man with a passion for God. His life and ministry reflect his heart for righteousness, holiness, and desire to see lives deeply impacted and transformed by the power of the gospel.

His book *The Spirit of Cain* will help you identify areas where you can gain greater victory over the work of the enemy in your life. Understanding the root of sin in our lives can help us overcome it in greater ways. Andrew's book will give you fresh insights into how you can live a victorious Christian life. I wholeheartedly recommend this book!"

—Barry Raeburn
Barry Raeburn Evangelistic Association
www.barryraeburn.org

"Andrew walks with an integrity that's rare these days! He's one of the purest human beings I know! I feel like that's why he is the perfect person to write *The Spirit of Cain*. Andrew allows Jesus to be himself. That's why I feel God has trusted him with such revelation!"

—Charles Jones
Musician and worshiper

THE SPIRIT OF CAIN

BREAKING FREE FROM JEALOUSY,
INSECURITY, AND UNHEALTHY COMPETITION

ANDREW BILLINGS

The Spirit of Cain: Breaking Free from Jealousy, Insecurity, and Unhealthy Competition

Copyright © 2015 Andrew Billings

ISBN-13: 978-099691940-1

All rights reserved. No part of this book may be reproduced in any form, except for brief quotations in printed reviews, without permission in writing from the author.

Contact the author at www.andrewbillings.org.

Unless otherwise identified, Scripture quotations are taken from the New King James Version. Copyright © 1982 by Thomas Nelson, Inc. Used by permission. All rights reserved. Scripture quotations marked KJV are taken from the King James Version.

Printed in the United States of America

Dedication

This book is dedicated to the much-needed establishing of greater unity in the wider body of Christ. It is dedicated to agreement with the prayer that Jesus prayed:

> "I do not pray for these alone, but also for those who will believe in Me through their word; that they all may be one, as You, Father, are in Me, and I in You; that they also may be one in Us, that the world may believe that You sent Me. And the glory which You gave Me I have given them, that they may be one just as We are one."
>
> —John 17:20–22

ACKNOWLEDGEMENTS

I would like to honor my amazing wife, Rebekah, who has been a great strength, encourager, and support through the process of writing this book. You truly are a Proverbs 31 woman with a heart of pure gold. I love you very much.

I also honor Holy Spirit, Jesus, and my Father in heaven. Thank you for this revelation that can open our eyes to the traps and snares of the enemy in this area, and teach us to live more like Jesus. You wrote this book, and I am privileged to have merely held the pen. I love you, and it is my honor to live for you.

CONTENTS

Introduction: **MEET CAIN** 13

Chapter 1: **THE MOTIVE TO MURDER** 19

Chapter 2: **PARADISE WAS NOT ENOUGH** 31

Chapter 3: **THE SPIRIT OF CAIN** 47

Chapter 4: **THE STORY OF
JACOB AND HIS DESCENDANTS** 65

Chapter 5: **A THREATENED KING** 77

Chapter 6: **THE MAKING OF A MUTINY** 95

Chapter 7: **ENVY KILLS THE SON** 109

Chapter 8: **OVERCOMING THE SPIRIT OF CAIN** .123

Chapter 9: **INNER IDENTITY AND HUMILITY** 141

Chapter 10: **A KINGDOM WITH
NO EVIL COMPETITION** 157

Introduction

MEET CAIN

I grew up in the church, which means I saw a lot of things regarding relationships within the church. There was always someone trying to be better than another, someone trying to be more holy than someone else, and a person with a holier-than-thou approach. If you have been in church for any length of time, then you have probably experienced this too. Why couldn't everyone just want to love God and each other, believing the best in total innocence? Even though I saw many people who honored and loved each other as God commanded all of us to do, I also saw many people who had the common denominator of being driven to be the best they could possibly be. Not only that, but they were driven to be better than their brothers and sisters in Christ.

THE SPIRIT OF CAIN

When I was around twenty-three years old, I experienced a situation where my eyes were opened to the dangers of competition and ambition on a far more intentional level. While I was spending time loving on Jesus, enjoying the presence of God, in a new church plant I was a part of in Auckland, New Zealand, I had an interaction with a young man that I have never forgotten. At the end of the service, this young man walked up to me and began to say something really bizarre, completely taking me by surprise.

"You see that jacket you're wearing?" he asked. He was referring to a sports blazer I wore to church some weeks.

I replied, "Yes. It's my favorite one."

Arrogantly, he replied, "God told me that is going to be mine one day."

Of course I was uncomfortable with this whole situation, even agitated by the fact that he would be so forceful in his statement that he was going to own my jacket one day. Part of the reason I was perturbed was because I could feel the jealousy that was emanating from him, making it difficult for me to respond to him in a Christlike way. So I simply backed away from the conversation the best way I knew how, doing as much as I could to be gracious to him.

When I thought about what he said to me later on, I realized there was far more being said in his statement than that he simply wanted my jacket. Envy was present in his heart, but not just for my jacket. There was envy of what he perceived I had in the way of my calling and favor from the Lord. He didn't realize that in his own identity with God, everything I had was available to him as well. Though I did not fully understand it at the time, I could feel an overly competitive air boldly pressing against me as he told me God was going to give him my jacket.

As I walked away from that awkward situation, God clearly spoke to me in a way I did not expect to hear Him and had not heard anything like it before. He said, "Be careful or that relationship will be like Cain and Abel." God was warning me that there was more present than met the eye. He would later reveal to me the desperate ambition present in this young man that would personally compete against me over the years to come. There was an alarm that went through my spirit, though I didn't fully understand what God meant right then.

This interaction was just the beginning of a revelation from the Lord that would take years to uncover and learn. Since the conversation I had that day and what God later spoke to my heart, I have seen many examples of envy and competition present within the body of Christ. God began to speak to me about a spirit that is present within the church, and that I hadn't heard about at the time—the spirit of Cain.

As time went on I want to assure you that I kept my coat, and I also began to see the outworking of something that was so jealous and competitive within the people of God. This man used me as a benchmark to beat in terms of spiritual growth, fruit, and ministry. Throughout the years following that interaction with him, I would experience many other instances of character assassination, all with the motive to gain advantage, position, or favor with leaders we were serving. However, I never forgot the warning from the Lord that day. In fact, that very warning has kept me safe in this area as God has led and navigated my life through some tumultuous relationships.

THE SPIRIT OF CAIN

We must not be naïve to demonic spirits, as their agenda will never be in our favor. They are at war with us. The kingdom of hell is set against the sons and daughters of heaven; we can overcome the power of the enemy if we stand in the power of God's might and stay vigilant against the attacks of the enemy. We need to be aware of how the devil tries to work in the body of Christ. And we need to be aware of how he tries to work in our own hearts.

Jesus conquered the devil once and for all at the cross, but we must become as wise as serpents and harmless as doves when it comes to living the Christian life in this world. The enemy must not take advantage of us. Paul reminded the Corinthians that he didn't want Satan to "take advantage of us; for we are not ignorant of his devices" (2 Corinthians 2:11). Many people, like Abel before us, do not see this spirit coming and have trouble knowing the right way to respond when it rears its ugly head. The spirit of Cain is nothing more than a demonic spirit.

This book has been written with the intent to bring exposure to the spirit of Cain, which goes unnoticed much of the time in the body of Christ. It is my desire to bring an understanding of its nature and how it works in our midst. But, most importantly, I have written to show you how to defeat it in Jesus Christ, by His blood and through the power of the Holy Spirit. My prayer is that as you read this book, the Holy Spirit would open your spiritual eyes to clearly see and be equipped so that you can be free of this spirit, both from around you and from being in you. There is no place for competition and jealously in the body of Christ.

We are going to take a journey through history and look at how this wicked deception, condition, and spirit has been sown into the very fabric of our psychological DNA from infancy, then strategically used by the enemy to displace and divide our lives, relationships, and the call of God upon us. We are going to look at this common thread through a consistent manifestation of it in so many great stories recorded in the Word of God. And we are also going to see the root causes of this human flaw and how we can defeat it and be free of it in our lives.

In order to become wiser and more aware of the strategies of the devil in this area, we must look back through time to see more clearly the spirit that has preceded many counts of death and destruction from the world's inception. There is a demonic blood trail of these symptoms throughout the history of time and recorded for us in Scripture. Once we can see this spirit at work more clearly, we will be better alerted to the telltale signs of this spirit in our world today, and begin to raise a higher standard against it in our lives, relationships, churches, and even workplaces and business organizations. God has given us all we need to defeat the spirit of Cain.

Chapter 1

THE MOTIVE TO MURDER

There is something that I have observed in the heart of people over the years, something that is innate in the human condition and that contends to want to be better or have more than our neighbor. Who has the best car, who earns the most money in their job, and who has the nicest house on the block are all common areas we try to compete in.

We can all be great in our individual callings and pursuits, walking in excellence and favor in all the things we do. But this should never be a determining valuation of who we are as people in the body of Christ. At the same time, however, any resentment of others toward our successes should never discourage us from excelling. God designed us to succeed and be great, saying to

THE SPIRIT OF CAIN

Adam, "Be fruitful and multiply; fill the earth and subdue it; have dominion over the fish of the sea, over the birds of the air, and over every living thing that moves on the earth" (Genesis 1:28). God has set it in the heart of man to do well, but, unfortunately, sin has perverted and corrupted that desire.

Do you remember that kid in class who was so insecure that he drove himself to be an achiever in order to find affirmation? While growing up, I remember kids in my own class who would sabotage other kids' projects and assignments to eliminate the competition so they could win first place. Although this is seen as not being kind—it just looked like a kid being cruel or heartless, something they would eventually grow out of—there was so much more beneath the surface of the mere act of sabotaging another kid's project.

This whole concept of competition is so deeply rooted in our human nature that it is often passed off as normal or a personality trait, because, after all, everyone wants to be the best, right? The desire to do well is good and often comes from God, but the whole concept of cutting others down to get there is downright disturbing. If we stop just long enough to think about it, what was so easily demonstrated in a young child becomes more sophisticated as they grow up. Success is great, but heart motive is so much more important in how we achieve that success.

Unhealthy competition is a key catalyst to division and strife being created in any environment. The gateway to an open heaven is unity, which is the nemesis of unhealthy competition. The spirit of Cain dictates that I want what you have and I am not secure or satisfied with myself because what you have makes me feel insufficient or incomplete. In order to regain security and satisfaction in my life, therefore, I must compete against you by any means necessary, and I must win by any way I possibly can.

Not only is this competition present in our culture, but it has crept into the culture of the church as well. Instead of competing for material things, like wanting to have the nicest car or house, we want to be the person who is the most anointed or who has the most visible gifts. James and John came to Jesus one day and wanted to know if He would do for them what they were about to ask. When Jesus asked what it was they wanted Him to do, they said, "Grant us that we may sit, one on Your right hand and the other on Your left, in Your glory" (Mark 10:37). They wanted a position of power. They wanted to be set above the other disciples. They weren't satisfied with what they had—being two of the twelve who walked with Jesus day in and day out—they wanted something more.

This is no small subject we are dealing with here. Evil competition is a huge tear in the bride's wedding dress. We must allow healing and repentance to come so Jesus can return to a glorious book-of-Acts bride and not one who has cut off parts of her own limbs. We are one body—eyes, ears, feet, and arms—which means we need each other to function properly. When we are competing against one another, we are fighting against our own body. How is Jesus glorified in that? How can a church be healthy when it is attacking itself? It simply can't.

In order to banish the spirit of Cain from the house of God, we must destroy and banish this spirit first from our own personal hearts and lives. As true sons and daughters in the kingdom of God, we each individually have our own identity and call, then we are part of the larger body collectively. If each one of us has been called by the Lord to do something specific within the body of Christ particularly and society at large, then why do we look at someone else's call, identity, or anointing to use as a benchmark or level to beat?

The answer to this question is simple. The reason we look to other peoples' call and gifts is because we have not found our own special identity and call in the Father's love due to a lack of intimacy with Him. Because of this lack of intimacy with God, we look insecurely at others in jealousy, which makes us feel even more lacking, so we end up despising that person and the seed of competition is sown. The end result of this will only end up in hurt, damage, further insecurity, and eventual rejection.

Adam and Eve's first two sons each brought an offering before the Lord. Since Cain was a tiller of the ground, he brought an offering to the Lord from the fruit of the ground. Abel, however, was a keeper of sheep, so he brought to the Lord one of the sheep from his flock. The Bible says that "the LORD respected Abel and his offering, but He did not respect Cain and his offering. And Cain was very angry, and his countenance fell" (Genesis 4:4–5).

Cain became hurt by the rejection of God's acceptance of Abel's offering. He never based his identity on his intimacy with God, so Cain looked at Abel through the eyes of competition rather than through the eyes of love. Because Abel's offering was accepted and Cain's was not, the seed of hatred was sown in Cain's heart. The seed continued to grow larger and larger until one day they were walking in the field, and Cain decided to rise up against Abel and kill him. The seed of hatred resulted in the first murder that ever took place in the creation of the world.

THE MOTIVE TO MURDER

It is good to desire the best in life and in God—we have been created to excel and soar. But our motive to excel should be set on God, not on how God is using or blessing those around us. Cain became jealous of Abel not because Abel's offering was better than Cain's, but because of the affirmation and love Abel received from the Lord. Abel's heart was right in giving his offering to the Lord.

The first murder in history could have been avoided if Cain would have corrected his heart and not competed with his brother for God's affections. If Cain had sought the heart of God, receiving his own love and affirmation from his relationship with God, then it would have been a different story. God even tried to warn Cain of this, saying, "Why are you angry? And why has your countenance fallen? If you do well, will you not be accepted? And if you do not do well, sin lies at the door. And its desire is for you, but you should rule over it" (Genesis 4:6–7).

A friend of mine really struggled in this area for a number of years. I observed him over a period of many years, as this unhealthy competition would display itself in his life and in various relationships he had. Whenever someone around him began to excel in a specific area, I would watch him engage the situation or conversation, trying to outdo the person who was doing well. I began to see beneath the layers of what was really going on inside his heart. There was a desperate need for attention and affirmation that was present within him, and there was a great void of identity. This caused him to lunge into situations with all his energy, trying to be seen as just as good as, if not better than, the next person, rather than celebrating another person's victories or the position God raised him or her into.

THE SPIRIT OF CAIN

This became more apparent when he was given a position in a church that placed him as second in charge. The thing that shocked me the most was that I watched him not be content with his place and role, but he became contentious for the one position above him, not recognizing that he was not gifted or called to stand in that role at that time. Rather, he was equipped to support that role during that specific season of his life.

Competition can become an evil thing in the heart of humanity because it abandons being quietly content with where God has you and what God has given to you. It drives you in your own fleshly strength toward jealousy and striving for more than you have. It is basically the vehicle people use to obtain their lusts and ungodly desires.

The word *competition* comes from the word *compete*, in which all parties dual for the crown in various aspects of life. In order to compete, there must be an opponent or opposition to compete against, which in the heat of the struggle becomes an enemy standing between the competitor and the prize. This is where the problem begins.

Absalom, who was King David's son, desired what his father had, not being content with the position he was given. He became jealous and envious of his father, then the seeds of "I can do a better job" or "that person doesn't deserve that, I do" and "I should have the throne" began to take root in his heart. This root then justified the actions that followed. He would go out every day and sit at the gate of the city. When people would be on their way to see the king, he would say, "The king is too busy; let me take care of you." Once enough people were reliant on and affirming Absalom, beginning to swear more allegiance

THE MOTIVE TO MURDER

to him than King David, that was when he made his move to make himself king.

The object of competition becomes more than just a benchmark that has to be beat. It becomes the opponent and the enemy being fought against. War will inevitably break out when the spirit of Cain is in operation. Many church leaders and business people have experienced this satanic form of treachery. This is the sin that unhealthy competition creates—it empowered Absalom to leave his position and ranking, choosing to establish a mutiny against true God-ordained authority.

And this is what empowered Cain to feel justified in killing Abel. The depraved sin nature can never be satisfied with current position or possessions; it's that constant lust for who another is or what he or she has that constantly drives them to trample on others in order to get ahead in life. This spiritual sin turns the environment of relationship into a battle zone motivated by a false perception of injustice or a lack of recognition that is fueled with the ugly sin of pride.

James writes of these very issues:

> Where do wars and fights come from among you? Do they not come from your desires for pleasure that war in your members? You lust and do not have. You murder and covet and cannot obtain. You fight and war. Yet you do not have because you do not ask. You ask and do not receive, because you ask amiss, that you may spend it on your pleasures. Adulterers and adulteresses! Do you not know that friendship with the world is enmity with God? Whoever therefore wants to be a friend of the

world makes himself an enemy of God. Or do you think that the Scripture says in vain, "The Spirit who dwells in us yearns jealously"? But He gives more grace. Therefore He says: "God resists the proud, but gives grace to the humble."

—JAMES 4:1–6

In light of this unhealthy competition, this Scripture puts a clear spotlight on the root motives and mind-sets found in this evil ambition.

The thing that marvels me the most about unhealthy competition is that it begins in childhood as something that most don't really see as problematic in nature. I remember playing on the school soccer team when I was around eight years old. There were more people on the team than players allowed on the field, so there was an intense rivalry for who would get onto the field to play the other team each week. It got so intense that some of the players started calculating ways to disqualify other team members so they could get to play.

This happened to me one week. A person on the team told our coach that I had said some bad thing that I had not said, and I was disqualified from playing that week. This particular person laughed at me as he ran out to play in the position I was supposed to play that day. We were supposed to be a team, putting our best players on the field for each given scenario, allowing strengths of individually talented players to shine in unique and necessary ways for the benefit of the whole team. But instead of being focused on the team, each player was trying to get ahead by turning against his teammates.

THE MOTIVE TO MURDER

Unhealthy competition is either motivated by jealousy or ambition. A strange aspect of looking at this condition that leads to sin starts with a small level of jealousy and lust and it ends with a form of murder. Jesus said that if we hate our brother, then we have murdered him already in our heart (Matthew 5:21–22). Sin always starts in the heart. And if it is left in the heart unchecked, that root of evil will eventually make its ways to the outside of our world in a physical way. This negative attribute is rife in our culture. It is the age-old story of "you have something that I want, so now you are no longer my friend or companion. You are the obstacle that I must remove in order to take what you have, or, at the very least, to topple you from your position. If I can't have it, then neither should you."

The story of jealously and rivalry has penned the tale of countless millions of lives throughout history. From it have come broken friendships, feuds, rivalries, murders, and all kinds of wars—even genocide is the result of this spirit. Just look at Ishmael and Isaac. One was the son of the bondwoman and the other the son of the free woman. Although Ishmael was born through Abraham's foolish actions, he was not the son of promise (it is possible that his mother told him that story while growing up). And I can only imagine the rejection and jealousy that must have been kindled in Ishmael's heart. That which is born of the flesh wars against that which is born of the spirit (Galatians 5:17).

Jack Coe was a preacher and healing evangelist in the 1940s and '50s who sought a ministry of the Lord's divine healing after encountering the miraculous through his own life. After Coe became a born-again Christian and turned his life around, he

THE SPIRIT OF CAIN

became determined to preach the gospel of Jesus Christ. As a bold man, he enjoyed healing and casting out demons too.

When he first started out serving in a church, he asked the pastor of a local Church of God if he could preach. When the pastor of the church told him he could work at the altar instead, Coe left insulted. The Lord told him to go back and do anything the minister asked of him, so Coe went back. When the pastor gave Coe custodial duties, he left again. After a night of tossing and turning, he returned to that church to work as a custodian. Coe's loyalty gave him the opportunity to work up from Sunday school teacher to the role of associate pastor.

Eventually, Jack began to pursue tent meetings, which were a popular venue for traveling preachers and evangelists during that era. In one of his first tent meetings, Jack Coe asked God to fill it with people. The Lord told Jack that He would fill the tent if he had faith and gave God the glory. At one point in his life, Coe became such a high-demand healing evangelist that he would stay up all night praying for the sick, which really caused his own health to deteriorate. At this time in Coe's life, the Lord told him he needed to rest, so Coe sold all of his possessions and lived on the road.

While on the road, Jack Coe told the people he needed a large amount of money or creditors would take his truck away. After a wealthy woman wrote a check for the full amount he needed, Jack asked the people for some type of musical instrument to contribute to his revival tent. After Coe published his own *Herald of Healing* magazines, he decided that he wanted to have the largest tent revival meeting in America. Oral Roberts, who was a well-known man of God for faith and miracles, highly respected

Jack Coe and was even quoted as calling him "a great man of faith." Jack attended an Oral Roberts meeting not wanting to be outdone by any other ministers; he just wanted to measure Roberts' tent to make sure the one he ordered was bigger. So Coe had a tent custom made to seat twenty-two thousand people and required three tractor-trailers to transport it.

Coe was never satisfied with what God was doing in his life. His boasting and competition was because of undisputed greed for more. He never dealt with it in his early walk with the Lord, so when he was older it rose up and showed itself. He would sometimes speak of other evangelists' tent meetings as being merely "pup tents."

It is said by some that Dr. Kenneth E. Hagin, founder of the Word of Faith movement, talked to Jack Coe and warned him prophetically after the Lord spoke to Hagin about Coe. Dr. Hagin warned Coe that unless he judged himself in three areas—his love for the body of Christ, his weight problem, and his love of money—then he would leave the earth early. Some suggest he was warned about competition also. Jack Coe didn't take heed to what the Lord had warned him about so many times early on in his life and ministry. And it appears that he was called to go home at the young age of thirty-eight and be with the Lord after being diagnosed with polio in 1956.

If you are saved, then you are a son or daughter of promise. But God has warned us that if we compare ourselves with ourselves, then we are unwise. We are to never allow ourselves to compare our gifting or position or anointing with another one of God's sons or daughters. This is not a competition in which every man is out for himself, to prove his own worth or identity; this is

THE SPIRIT OF CAIN

like the army that Joel saw, the army that stands side by side and does not break rank in the midst of battle (Joel 2:7–8).

There is of course a healthy competition in which elements of competing cause people to be pushed to give more in order to raise their performance, which encourages growth and higher excellence. But I am not referring to that type of competition here; rather, I am isolating the unhealthy aspect of competition that begins to see other people as a threat or obstacle to get to the top.

We must always be prepared to examine our own thoughts and intents to make sure that we are walking in the Spirit and not in the flesh. If we are walking in the flesh—even subtly—then on some level we may be walking in unhealthy competition and warring against the Spirit of God who lives within us. This may not be our intention, but our hearts are most deceitfully wicked things at times. Jeremiah writes, "The heart is deceitful above all things, and desperately wicked; who can know it?" (Jeremiah 17:9).

The reality is that the moment we take our eyes off of Jesus, we are looking at people by which to measure our lives. It is true that sometimes we don't understand our own intentions and thoughts, but God is faithful to show us what is there if we will simply ask Him. We can truly be free from selfish ambition and unhealthy competition through the power and blood of Jesus Christ.

Chapter 2

PARADISE WAS NOT ENOUGH

Even though I'm using the term *spirit of Cain*, we can see another example of this spirit at work before Cain was even born. Before the earth was ever created, the spirit of jealousy and covetousness and rivalry exemplified itself in Satan being thrown out of heaven. Although the spirit of Cain never possessed Lucifer, this trait can be seen in Lucifer, helping us to learn much from the story of his fall from heaven. We can watch the same cycle operate and evolve in the mind of Lucifer, keeping perspective that we are not looking at a mutiny but rather the process of coveting that caused Satan to be cast out of heaven.

Let's go back to the very beginning, even before the "in the beginning" in Genesis 1:1. Let's go back to before the earth was

THE SPIRIT OF CAIN

created, to the time when Lucifer was beautiful, serving at the foot of God's throne, before he was evil, before he was ever called Satan. Lucifer was quite possibly the most beautiful creature in heaven (except God Himself), the most beautiful in all of God's creation. Ezekiel tells of this time:

> Son of man, take up a lamentation for the king of Tyre, and say to him, "Thus says the Lord God: 'You were the seal of perfection, full of wisdom and perfect in beauty. You were in Eden, the garden of God; every precious stone was your covering: the sardius, topaz, and diamond, beryl, onyx, and jasper, sapphire, turquoise, and emerald with gold. The workmanship of your timbrels and pipes was prepared for you on the day you were created. You were the anointed cherub who covers; I established you; you were on the holy mountain of God; you walked back and forth in the midst of fiery stones. You were perfect in your ways from the day you were created, till iniquity was found in you. By the abundance of your trading you became filled with violence within, and you sinned; therefore I cast you as a profane thing out of the mountain of God; and I destroyed you, O covering cherub, from the midst of the fiery stones. Your heart was lifted up because of your beauty; you corrupted your wisdom for the sake of your splendor; I cast you to the ground, I laid you before kings, that they might gaze at you. You defiled your sanctuaries by the multitude of your iniquities, by the iniquity of your trading; therefore I brought

PARADISE WAS NOT ENOUGH

fire from your midst; it devoured you, and I turned you to ashes upon the earth in the sight of all who saw you.'"

—Ezekiel 28:12–18

There was a time when Lucifer worshiped only God, a time he orchestrated and led all of heaven in worship toward God in absolute purity and innocence. He was in a most-trusted position of leading all the hosts of heaven to praise God, being allowed close to the throne of the King. Can you imagine how amazing and beautiful things were during that time?

Lucifer's heart was slowly perverted by his own beauty and confidence in himself, however. His only job was to channel and direct all of the incoming worship and glory of heaven straight to the throne and person of God. But as each day passed, he developed a lust for what was rightfully God's. Even though this is the only instance that sin has ever taken place inside heaven, we can see that it sprung from this evil competition in the heart of Lucifer.

Lucifer's position and job description was that of a servant, not a king. He constantly watched the glory of God each day in heaven, and each day he somehow grew more familiar with God and more forgetful of his rank and role, the position God had given him close to His throne. Lucifer's heart began to yearn for the glory and worship that he directed from the hosts of heaven toward the throne, and he began to like the way it felt. He wanted it for himself. The great self-deception had commenced to poison Lucifer's heart. He became more enamored with himself, his beauty, his gifting, and his abilities. At the same time, a gradual

THE SPIRIT OF CAIN

resentment evolved into a deep hatred of God, thus causing him to ultimately be thrown out of heaven.

A jealous rivalry, envy, and competition emerged in the heart of Lucifer, which changed the gearing mechanism from a spirit-of-Cain type of heart condition to an outworking of a rebellious public mutiny, the Luciferian spirit in which angels other than himself were drawn into the sentiment. This jealous rivalry grew inside him and became his main focal point, until, in his case, it became external and he led a mutiny, which then became what we now know to be the spirit of Lucifer, possessing the hallmark statement, "I will arise." Lucifer was not possessed, but the spirits that we are now faced with as humans originated in the heart of Lucifer in this devastating fall.

If jealousy, envy, and competition are not dealt with, they will inevitably look to express themselves in and through our hearts. It may be in an individual rising up, as Cain did with Abel, or it may evolve into a public and open stance or assault against the authority of the Lord. Satan did not rise up on his own to strike God like Cain did to Abel; rather, he gathered an army like Absalom did against his father, David. Only the first part of Lucifer's story applies to the spirit of Cain, and the psychological process that evolved in his unchecked heart led to this massive change on the course of history in both heaven and earth.

The irony is that God had entrusted Lucifer with one of the most notable positions in heaven. But Lucifer was not content in his honored place, especially since millions of angels that occupied and served in heaven were mostly below Lucifer in rank. He still found a reason to become envious of God and discontent with who and where he was, rather than thankful for the honor given to him.

Lucifer's sin began with the seed of pride—pride in who he was and what he was able to do. He lost his adoration and desire to please God and became self-confident. In this frame of mind, he was beginning to explore his thought life and questioned God's deserved worship, while at the same time starting to enjoy the taste of worship for himself. This evolved from a mere fleeting thought into more of a meditation of his heart. And from there it became something that his mind was obsessed with. Lucifer actually began to believe his own madness of thinking that he could possibly have what God had, that he, the created, was equal or superior to the Creator. It was at this time that scheming was now well underway, and what he thought was a master plan to overthrow God was embedded into his being.

Up until this point in time, Lucifer had not verbalized what was working in his heart, as we understand it to be. All of this was thoughts he was having, all of them internal. But it had progressed from a crazy thought that quickly went through his mind into a strong alternate reality delusion. Once Lucifer started to communicate his madness to the angels that looked up to him, it became something else and transitioned into what we know as the Luciferian spirit, in which this sentiment was spread like bitterness and defiled many. Ultimately, a mutinous war broke out in heaven, resulting in Satan being cast out.

The deception was so great that it then spread beyond Lucifer's heart and went throughout the ranks of the angels in heaven. Misery needs company; it needs support. The division that followed was that the angels chose sides. A great war in heaven inevitably followed—the angels that fought alongside Lucifer would soon be cast out. Jesus told His disciples after they excitedly came back from casting out demons, that He saw Satan fall like lightening from heaven (Luke 10:18), thus referring to this war in heaven.

Satan's war looked like a child's tantrum from God's perspective on the throne. I can just see God the Father raise His hand and point His finger, releasing His resounding thundering voice that shook heaven and defeated Satan and his rebellion in a single moment. I wonder if the flashes of lightning around the throne flew out and struck the once-pure but now perverted worship leader, banishing him to the earth. And all because of competition for what God has and is.

We all intimately know sin in this world because it was born in the heart of a created angel that became intoxicated and obsessed with what God had, going to extreme lengths to strike out at the King of heaven in a foolishly driven attempt to be king himself. Lucifer had hated the person of God because He was seated in the position that he ultimately wanted. The hatred toward God was most likely less about hatred for who God was, but rather hatred toward God because of what He had and where He sat.

Jealousy, envy, and competition are far less about the person and always more about what they have. In fact, in most cases, the haters lose perception of the individual and are drunk in their quest to either rob or dethrone the envied person. It is a deception that is actually grounded in lies of false reality. And it gives the delusion that something can be taken and not earned, disrespecting the individual's reward for their earned success, favor, or position.

The fall of Lucifer from heaven led to another fall that has

PARADISE WAS NOT ENOUGH

affected humanity ever since the time of Adam and Eve. Adam and Eve made a decision when they were both tempted: would they want to be like God, knowing good *and* evil, or would they be satisfied with the likeness of God they already possessed? We need to look at why, in the midst of a perfect paradise, they were discontent with their position and began to pursue to be like God, after hearing such a strong warning from God Himself.

"In the day that you eat the fruit, you will be like God," Satan said through the serpent. Contrary to what most of us have always assumed, the act of eating the fruit was more than mere curiosity for Adam and Eve. Prior to eating from the Tree of the Knowledge of Good and Evil, Adam and Eve were human beings in the state of perfect creation, something none of us have experienced since that time. Their state of existence and awareness of God was elevated far above our current awareness.

It is a well-established fact that the human brain is only used at approximately 10 percent of its actual capacity. I do not believe for a second that God created the brain for the extra 90 percent unless it was not supposed to be used. Prior to the fall, Adam and Eve may very well have used the full extent of their brains, while after the fall there was a shift in their brain power, as sin began to degenerate their now-mortal bodies. We have no idea how long they lived in Eden before the fall, but they were on some level immortal—they were created to live forever in perfection.

God warned them that in the day they ate of the fruit, they would surely die, implying that dying was a foreign concept to them. When they ate the fruit, they did not actually die right away, but rather they began dying—decay began to work in their physical bodies. The immediate death they experienced was spiritual, being completely cut off from God because of their sin. The act of eating the fruit was not that of mere interest or curiosity—it was much more than that.

The fruit was more than a mere physical appeal to the appetite. There were two trees that are mentioned in the Garden of Eden, the Tree of Life and the Tree of the Knowledge of Good and Evil. The Tree of Life, for instance, was an actual tree that was producing fruit that emanated life. This was not an orange tree; it was a tree bearing fruit, which we have never since seen. The fruit was life, and as they ate it they lived. God had also commanded them concerning the Tree of the Knowledge of Good and Evil, that in the day they ate of it they would surely die. Again, this also was no apple tree. It bore fruit that had spiritually active content.

One tree gave them life and the other forbidden fruit promised death. Adam and Eve at this point did not know evil, but they also did not know good. There was some amazing shroud of innocence on them that caused them to know nothing of anything bad or evil, but at the same time they did not know what was good either. They were covered in the glory of God. Rather than being aware of good and evil, they lived in a perfect state of existence in the presence of God. Their life was holistic and peaceful. Unfortunately, as we know from reading the first few chapters of Genesis, they disobeyed and fell. But why?

One of the points that was included in the sin of them eating the fruit was, like Lucifer before them who said, "I will arise," Adam and Eve also became delusional and for a brief time were convinced that they would somehow become like God. They were essentially competing with God, given that "they would be like Him" and not need Him anymore, even though they were already created in His image and likeness. God was seen as a peer or a rival.

The evil competition that is so prevalent in our culture today, and even within the body of Christ, stems right back to the beginning of humanity. Not only that, but its fruit is always death, destruction, and division. Little did Adam and Eve consider that when they ate from the Tree of the Knowledge of Good and Evil they lost access to the Tree of Life and began to die. If we really consider the serpent possessed by the devil as he pitched the sale of the idea of disobedience toward God, he was really convincing Eve into the same delusion that he corrupted the angels with— competition and rebellion toward God.

All God had ever done was create humanity, build them a heavenly sanctuary called Eden, and love His creation as friends. And here, in this place, we see the beginnings of how the spirit of Cain works—it competes against the innocent and those who have done right. It breeds discontent with what we have because we see that someone else has more, or is more favored, or is more blessed.

I will take the risk and speculate that as the serpent spoke, Eve became envious of who God was and what God had. She wanted to become like Him. And that was what caused jealously and envy to arise in her heart, making her unsatisfied with what she had, thus causing her to eat of the forbidden fruit. James was right when he wrote, "For where envy and self-seeking exist, confusion and every evil thing are there" (James 3:16).

Cain, the infamous son of Adam and Eve, was the first

murderer in the entire history of humanity. And the sin of Cain was the first time God ever came and warned a person before the actual act was committed. God did not even do this when the serpent was talking to Eve—He didn't step in and tell her not to eat of it again, somehow reemphasizing the results of what would happen if she chose to disobey. Rather, there was the one warning and that was it. But with Cain, God stepped in and warned him because he knew that competition was present in his heart. But why did he murder? Where did it all go wrong, and why did he resort to such extreme measures against his own flesh and blood? The person he should have protected the most—his brother, Abel—he killed because of envy and jealousy.

Cain never grasped the true nature of the fall his parents had. Maybe he even had an offense toward God through hearing about the sin, fall, and eviction from the Garden. He must have heard about the justice and great mercy of God the Father, the friend his parents knew so well. In many ways Cain coveted the affection of God, and yet there still must have remained an orphan spirit of disconnection toward truly being intimate with God, as he was not yet born while Adam and Eve were in Eden. Cain was only born after his parents were evicted from the nurturing and tranquil life in the Garden of Eden, which included daily walks and fellowship with God. From there they were cast out into a harsh, sin-infected world in which Adam and all his descendants would have to work and labor by the "sweat of their own brow" to forge a life and provide for themselves just to survive.

All Cain ever knew aside from the stories of better times with God from Adam and Eve was the consequence of their disobedience, in which their actions attempted to compete and be equal with God. Cain's relationship and knowledge of God was entirely different than his parents' relationship and knowledge of God. Because of this, there must have been an overwhelming heritage of rejection and failure in regards to God and Eden, and yet at the same time a reaching toward the covenant of hope God established in the sacrifice of an innocent and spotless animal, as God had demonstrated in Eden on that fateful day.

It is here that we find the two sons of Adam and Eve becoming their own men. No longer in their parents' care, they were obviously providing for themselves, as we know they both had trades, jobs they were engaged in. The Bible states that Abel was a shepherd and Cain was a vegetable farmer. Both sons brought their offerings to God from the fruit of their profession, demonstrating that they must have understood God's ways in regards to atonement for sin and acceptance by God through sacrifice.

The Bible says:

> And in the process of time it came to pass that Cain brought an offering of the fruit of the ground to the LORD. Abel also brought of the firstborn of his flock and of their fat. And the LORD respected Abel and his offering, but He did not respect Cain and his offering. And Cain was very angry, and his countenance fell.
> —GENESIS 4:3–5

Both of the men brought a sacrifice to the Lord, but not both sacrifices were accepted by the Lord. This story would be easier to understand if they were both vegetable gardeners and

THE SPIRIT OF CAIN

one sacrificed an animal and the other vegetables. In this piece of history, however, we have Abel who sacrificed the way he had heard God sacrifice in Eden, and Cain sacrificed in the way he saw fitting out of a place of what he knew—vegetables and grain.

One of the men did right and was accepted by God, while the other did not do right because he sacrificed in his own way and on his own terms. Vegetables or grain could not shed blood and facilitate the remission of sins. Cain obviously had a different heart than Abel in that his heart was disconnected from God and was hard. Abel had innocence about him, a purity that didn't even see Cain's fury building.

I can imagine seeing Abel walking about his day-to-day routine, happy and blessed that God was pleased with him. Each day, through the eyes of fury and rage, and through a distorted jealousy, Cain would watch Abel. Each day that Cain watched Abel, his scorn and resentment grew. It started as a mild agitation, but it didn't stop there. Resentment turned into hatred, and hatred eventually turned into rage.

Even though Abel didn't see this coming, God did. He approached Cain and sought to connect with him and forewarn him to do what was right.

> So the LORD said to Cain, "Why are you angry? And why has your countenance fallen? If you do well, will you not be accepted? And if you do not do well, sin lies at the door. And its desire is for you, but you should rule over it."
>
> —GENESIS 4:4–7

Cain's countenance fell because his desire was to be accepted by the Lord. Rather than being accepted, however, Cain was rejected and not respected by the Lord. God encouraged Cain to do what was right, which would have been trading vegetables for a lamb and sacrificing that before the Lord. Obtaining a lamb and sacrificing it would have been an easy task for Cain, but now spite and rage consumed him, and Cain was driven toward evil against his very own brother.

I don't think Abel saw this coming, because, aside from the fact he was a great deal more innocent and God centered, he most likely did not understand the toxicity of poison that was eating and contaminating Cain's heart. It could have also been due to the fact that it seems Cain would have struck him down from behind. If Abel suspected Cain of doing evil, he would never have allowed him to get so close, become so vulnerable, and even possibly turn his back while Cain reached for the murder weapon.

Cain's initial desire was to be accepted by God, but that no longer was the focus of his heart. His focus had shifted from wanting to be accepted to now being consumed with jealousy and competition, which had overcome him. Murder, in his perspective, was the only option.

The Bible says that Cain murdered his brother in the field. But why did he do it in the field and not in front of the family living area or village? Understanding this provides a clearer perspective into the traits of this evil competition.

Cain slew Abel out in the field where no one else could see what was taking place. Like Joseph's brothers, their father, Israel, would not be able to see the treachery and would believe their

THE SPIRIT OF CAIN

story that a savage animal had killed him. Understanding the motives and structure of why this happened begins to reveal to us the sinister characteristics and outworking of the way evil competition will play out in its final stages of working through a person.

Assassinating the competition while still attempting to maintain an innocent appearance is a core characteristic of the spirit of Cain. We can see this in action by observing Cain's interaction with God after the murder. When God asked Cain where his brother was, it reveals just how cold and calculated Cain was at this point in his life—he was totally callous in his heart toward God. There was zero emotion or remorse, but rather that of someone now resolved to act like nothing took place and assuming innocence. Cain acted as if he knew nothing about the wickedness he had just carried out.

The consequence of Cain's sin brought about judgment and exile from the land that Adam and Eve lived in. On top of that, God put a mark on Cain that caused him to be despised by all people. We clearly see here that not only is there a consequence but there is a curse that results from living and operating in the spirit of Cain. We can safely conclude that the treachery of taking this road will actually result in demotion, not promotion. The road that Cain took was not that of mere attempting to get a coveted blessing mixed with revenge, like he first perceived, but rather it was that of being totally stripped and distanced even further from the blessing. It is not a coincidence that the sin of Cain was the first recorded sin outside of Eden.

The traits I have just addressed begin to describe a very real demonic entity that has been at work in the earth ever since the fall of man up until this current day. The Holy Spirit told me this was the spirit of Cain that was at work. We are to be aware of it, and so protect our hearts by engaging in intimacy with the Lord.

Chapter 3

THE SPIRIT OF CAIN

One day as I was talking to the Lord about problems I was having around unhealthy competition coming from someone I knew, and all the issues that go along with that, God began to speak to me extensively about this demonic spirit, and He referred to this as "the spirit of Cain." He was not saying that Cain, the person, was in operation; rather, He told me that a demonic spirit was in operation in the same way that most Christian circles recognize a spirit of Jezebel as not the woman herself but a demonic spirit of manipulation, control, and witchcraft. Even though I had never heard this talked about before, nor even referred to, I began looking closer at it in the Scriptures. I discovered that there were more instances of evil competition, jealousy, and murder revealed in the Bible than other well-known spirits, like Jezebel, the false prophet manipulator, or the spirit of Absalom, the supplanting mutinous spirit.

What got into Cain's heart was a demon spirit, just in the same way the devil entered Judas before betraying Jesus. In the same way that the biblical character Jezebel from the time of Elijah is clearly recognized as operating in a demonic manipulative and controlling spirit, the Holy Spirit has revealed to me that Cain in the Bible has a spirit that still plagues the body of Christ today. The spirit of Cain is an evil and unhealthy competitive spirit, carrying envy, jealousy, and rivalry that thrives in those having insecurities, father wounds, rejection, pride, and selfish ambition. Make no mistake about it: this spirit is as dangerous as the Jezebel spirit.

After the two brothers had sacrificed to the Lord, and one was accepted and the other rejected, the character of the spirit of Cain was revealed by God. God may have actually appeared to Cain like He did with Abraham years later when He asked him, "Why are you angry? And why has your countenance fallen? If you do well, will you not be accepted? And if you do not do well, sin lies at your door. And its desire is for you, but you should rule over it" (Genesis 4:6–7). In the Amplified Version, it translates "sin crouches at your door." I find it fascinating that God Himself comes and graphically describes this spirit's nature and intent to Cain. If we pay attention here, we see God painting the portrait of this evil and sinister spirit lurking and hovering, even crouching, at the door of Cain's heart.

Close your eyes for a moment and picture the scene that followed, in which Cain slew his brother. Can you see him

THE SPIRIT OF CAIN

crouching or lying in wait for the perfect, opportune moment to attack Abel? This spirit is an opportunistic aggressive and predatory spirit that crouches and lies in wait for the perfect moment of vulnerability to strike at others who are more favored or have greater positions. It would be safe to say that Cain assumed the position of the spirit God described to him in the field as he himself commenced crouching for Abel's life.

It's important for us to see that God understands and describes to Cain the nature of this spirit. Because Cain refused to master the sin that crouched at his door, the sin actually mastered Cain as he assumed the stance of the described spirit and crouched for Abel's blood. Many times the spirit of Cain will be found in people who have a point to prove to themselves or others by succeeding and being the best so subliminally that they will finally find and experience value, worth, and acceptance, due to feeling inferior, disadvantaged, or jealous. Our true identity can only come from Father God, and getting it in any other way is going to be a disappointing counterfeit.

When we look at the way the two brothers brought their sacrifices before the Lord, Cain knew what the right thing to do was, and I'm sure Adam and Eve were articulate in how God went about the sacrifice for their sin of disobedience in the Garden. After all, God personally oversaw and carried out the first sacrifice immediately following the first sin. Adam and Eve must have watched in a state of shock, realizing the consequences of their disobedience as God took animals, killed them, and made Adam and Eve clothes from the skin. The skins were a covering to replace the man-made fig leaves. Adam and Eve would have known that a covering could only come as a result of a blood sacrifice. They would have told their boys many times around family fires at dinnertime how God killed an animal and made clothes for them. And yet Cain thought he could do things his own way.

Abel brought an offering of what he knew to be acceptable to the Lord. There is much to be learned in this statement. So many Christians today try to come to God on their own terms, creating the boundaries and terms of engagement with God based on their perception of what will work or what is achievable. And if they are not doing it God's way, then it won't be acceptable. No matter how much teaching about liberal grace is preached, people will not get through a loophole on this matter. Even God cannot stretch the rules to accept the unacceptable.

Oftentimes, these people become upset and resentful of folks who are offering what is right in and of their lives to the Lord as they discover that the Lord is not blessing what they are doing or how they are living in a self-assumed approach to God. Today, in the dispensation of grace we are currently living in, we are to present our bodies, our lives, as living sacrifices before the Lord.

The requirement of offerings and sacrifices has not changed; the only difference is now Jesus has become the Lamb of God who took away the sin of the world. However, we are still to live our lives as a sacrifice before the King, with our hearts as the altar. This will either cause favor, respect, promotion, and blessing to those who walk wisely before the King, or the opposite to those who do not, which would bring dishonor, disrespect, no promotion, stagnation, and no blessing. This is a very different result and can instigate the jealousy that seeded Cain to rise up and murder his brother.

THE SPIRIT OF CAIN

This spirit may be found in those with overzealous ambition to climb the ministry ladder or the hierarchy in the local church or ministry. It's good to want to do well, excel, and succeed in Christ, but the second that this identity of succeeding or surpassing others becomes part of the goal, then you will find that a person is willing to do almost anything to get there.

A person operating in the spirit of Cain will gladly grieve with those who experience pain and loss, because somehow there is an advantage in another being weakened by tragedy. And although there are levels of genuine sympathy for others in their time of grief, we will likely find a tear in the fabric of personality in that there is also a reveling and sadistic celebration in the demise or pain of others. But authentically rejoicing with those doing well is almost impossible for someone operating in this spirit.

Some of the most dangerous people who operate in this spirit are those who are passive-aggressive. These people easily become offended if they are not given recognition, positions, or promotions that they believe they deserve. The spirit of Cain presents everything as being fine, and usually some sort of political spirit will be present. Some people call this a good poker face or a political smile. But inwardly there is war in their heart that has grown from the seed of offense, a festering emotion that sees all other runners in their race as a threat to their survival.

The spirit of Cain is like a silent hunter who lurks in the shadows and cannot clearly be seen. It has an objective and is waiting for the prime moment to take advantage of a second of weakness or opportunity. It has a loaded gun but will not show it until the last minute. Or to put it more simply, God described it well through His prophet like this: "These people draw near with

THE SPIRIT OF CAIN

their mouths and honor Me with their lips, but have removed their hearts far from Me, and their fear toward Me is taught by the commandment of men" (Isaiah 29:13).

Sometimes the spirit of Cain will not so blatantly strike out. Rather, it will slowly set itself against Abel, slowly pulling the sticks out from the Jenga pile, undermining you or your position with the goal of obtaining that position for him- or herself. Like the steady but sure change of the temperature of boiling water, this spirit will begin to try and disqualify or discredit you over time, disdaining everything about you along the way while smiling and flattering you to your face.

To better understand and paint the picture of this spirit, let's look closer through the onion layers. A survival mentality is actually a dangerous one emotionally. Have you ever been or met a person trying to survive, especially from a financial perspective? These people are in a desperate situation and can become unstable in some aspects, with a mentality that is narrow and shortsighted. To get the money they do not have, it's not a want but a need to survive. Everyone else is no longer important—the only person who needs to survive is them.

In their view, they are at the top of the food chain and they are not moved by the consequences of putting themselves first, even if they have to fight to get there. They do not care if there are casualties along the way. I'm not talking about a hardworking person who is focused on making a living. Rather, I'm talking about either mentalities or situations that cause people to stop at nothing or no one to get what they desire.

The perfect example I can think of is one of the signs of the times that we live in. We can see these traits in shoppers

THE SPIRIT OF CAIN

in America on big sale holidays like Black Friday. People who have plenty of money and live well will stampede over the top of other shoppers to get to an item they want first when the store doors open, and not blink an eye if someone falls or is trampled to death. This frenzy takes place with people who actually don't need but rather want things so obsessively that human reason and decency can be discarded or temporarily forgotten.

This survival and selfish mentality is found in the spirit of Cain, an orphan spirit with selfish motives. And it also may have the appearance of a team player, but there are dark and hidden agendas below the surface—the opportune time will become a real and dangerous threat to others in one manifestation or another.

The spirit of Cain is looking out for what it can get for itself. It has a poverty mentality and lacks perspective. In the same way, it seems Cain did not understand that God had enough love and respect for both Abel and himself; his view was one of lack and poverty rather than one of perceiving the abundance of God's heart for both of them. And because of this, he felt driven to compete for God's love and attention.

Years ago I saw two men in a church who both had amazing administrative gifts. Over time I watched an unspoken rivalry become so intense as they jostled with each other to be the go-to guy for leadership in the church. I watched one of them in particular discredit and criticize the other, somehow presenting himself as the better man with more to offer. One would try to get closer to the senior pastor and try to become the preferred head usher and point of assistance—it was like watching that one overly aggressive person compete in a company for a promotion.

THE SPIRIT OF CAIN

I knew both of these men well, and there was plenty of room for both of them to function well in their own gifts together. But some unspoken perspective was driving things in this one man's heart to be the number one, rather than the number one team.

This spirit has the ability to wreak havoc in a team, business, or church environment. Like Jezebel and Absalom, the spirit of Cain will set itself against those the Lord has respected, promoted, or honored. Because Satan is at the root of all these spirits, and his agenda has not changed since his fall from heaven, they rebel against the anointed and war against authority. Paul tells us not to be naïve to the strategies of the enemy. If you are a pastor or leader, then read this carefully, as this may save you from a church split or serious fallout. I strongly advise you to study those you are considering for leadership in your church or business to see if this spirit is present within their heart, because, if it is, there will be trouble down the road unless the person is first set free.

Once the person has been consumed enough by the spirit of Cain, his or her conscience is no longer engaged—it is seared. They will not be listening anymore. Once they have given themselves over to jealousy and hatred, they have set themselves up to be instruments of the spirit of Cain. And at this point the person is quite comfortable with hating the Abel in their scenario; they have been positioned by the spirit of Cain and are just waiting for an opportunity to strike. And strike they will. I have witnessed this in our church more than once, where Cain uses the root of bitterness to validate a vengeful and murderous heart. We must take heed lest a root of bitterness spring up among us and defile us. There is much to be learned from the Scripture, "Not as Cain who was of the wicked one and murdered his brother. And why did he murder him? Because his works were evil and his brother's righteous" (1 John 3:12).

One of the clues criminal investigators always look for when putting together evidence at a crime scene is motive. Bitterness is the perfect candidate for Cain to have a motive. Sometimes bitterness can be blatant, while at other times it can be a subtle agitation of the heart that, if left unchecked or unforgiven, can grow slowly but surely into a monster living and directing the issues of a person's life. There was a man I knew for sixteen years who eventually succumbed to this spirit. Over the course of time, he moved to my city and became a part of our church. He led a home group of young men. After a few years had gone by, he was asked to preach every now and then. Over time we began to plan how we could raise him and his wife up to eventually become an associate pastor.

We started to place him into a role to see where his strengths lay and where areas that needed to be worked on were. But to do this we had to put him into a trusted position in which he began to be validated to the congregation as a pastoral leader. By this stage, I had been pastoring in our Orange County, California, church for a few years, and my wife and I were overseeing our church in New Zealand and raising up the team there too.

Being busy overseeing the two churches, I was not able to spend as much time as I used to with this man. I assured all of the team that no one was being neglected and to please understand the load on me was now restricting the amount of time I was able to spend with each of them. But I sensed this man pulling away from me, and so I made an effort to reach out to him and assure him of my love and commitment. He would tell me everything was fine and that he was working hard and loving his family well. But something didn't sit right with me in my spirit, so I became increasingly concerned over this, to the point that I eventually had to call a meeting with him.

In the meeting, he revealed his real heart toward me and began to make statements in which it was obvious that he had thought he deserved to be in charge of the church. He told me that I shouldn't have controlled him for so long, as well as many other accusations he brought against me, trying to twist my words. I was cut to the heart. This man was my friend and he had turned against me. I found out that almost a year earlier he felt like God had told him I was not for him, which was completely untrue. He even made remarks that he thought I was saying bad things about him behind the scenes, which I had never done. I was shocked hearing these words coming from his mouth, and I couldn't believe the deception that was in place. I pleaded and begged this long-time friend to hear me and reason with me because the statements he was making were not true. But he was determined to accuse me and act like he had been held back from a senior pastor role.

When I later discussed the conversation with my wife, who was present in the meeting, we began to see the trail of jealousy for our roles and that his ambition had blinded his heart toward us. We loved him and were actively looking to raise him up. But jealously had gotten a hold of his heart, causing envy to rise up. How had this long-time friend and fellow minister raise himself up against us with absolutely no outward sign of offense? How could he suddenly change and act as if he was aggressively our enemy?

THE SPIRIT OF CAIN

After that discussion I began to discover that this man had been gathering a great number of people from within the church and spreading his offenses, and it wasn't long after that he led a church split. I spent a great deal of time reflecting on this fast-moving outworking and began to see that it was not fast in the process at all. The spirit of Cain had been working for almost ten months before it manifested against me, eventually transitioning into an church split. In fact, I began to see the entire story of Cain and Abel play out in the year leading up to this sad point.

The tragic fact is that this story is far too common among churches, ministries, and even corporate and business environments than people most realize. The really scary thing is that in most cases the Cain spirit will have the person so convinced that they are on a campaign of justice. Because the seed of subtle competition or striving for position is so deeply rooted in the subconscious mind, people may not even know their own heart motives and will think that another reason is driving their campaign to rise up against their brother or sister, or their spiritual leader or coworker.

Jesus warned us that this level of deception would be prevalent when He said:

> These things I have spoken to you, that you should not be made to stumble. They will put you out of the synagogues; yes, the time is coming that whoever kills you will think that he offers God service. And these things they will do to you because they have not known the Father nor Me. But these things I have told you, that when the time comes, you may remember that I told you of them.

THE SPIRIT OF CAIN

And these things I did not say to you at the beginning, because I was with you.

—JOHN 16:1–4

"Where envy and self-seeking are...*every* evil thing is there" (James 3:16). This Scripture is a good insight into the spirit of Cain—behind it every evil sin will be found. Envy and self-seeking are two strongly evident hallmark traits found in Cain. And every evil thing includes murder. That may not mean physical murder, but it could be any form of character assassination or sabotaging your efforts in order to spite you.

For example, while watching government and presidential elections, I have been shocked to see a consistent trend that is widely accepted as normal. Public character assassination is almost cheered by the nation watching like blood sport was in the coliseum. It is the ultimate slaying of the opposition in order to get ahead and achieve more favor than his or her peers. Personal lives, past failures, and youthful mistakes that should remain confidential are dragged into the public eye, humiliating and shaming the opposition with the intent of disqualifying the other person running for office.

Although the spirit of Cain has many faces, some even sophisticated, the ultimate expression will be completely removing the perceived rival. Character assassination to the politician is what murder was to Cain, for it assumes a level of attempted negative control over another individual's life. It is a cunning facet of the spirit of Cain.

This is a very real demonic spirit that is carrying out the destructive intent of hell through anyone who will get in

THE SPIRIT OF CAIN

agreement with it. To outline the characteristics of the spirit of Cain more clearly, here are some of the most prevalent faces God has revealed to me:

- Cain is an orphan spirit.
- Cain is a poverty-minded spirit.
- Cain is an opportunistic spirit.
- Cain is an insincere spirit.
- Cain is a competitive spirit.
- Cain is a jealous spirit.
- Cain is a scheming spirit.
- Cain is a calculating spirit.
- Cain is a treacherous spirit.
- Cain is a vengeful spirit.
- Cain is a resentful spirit.
- Cain is a hating spirit.
- Cain is a murderous spirit.
- Cain is a coldhearted spirit.
- Cain claims injustice.

In this spirit you will see the same story that was played out in Cain's physical life, which includes people who are not genuinely happy for others who do well, who succeed, or who are promoted. But, rather, they are bitterly consumed with a jealous resentment that begins to look to disqualify the person as another is highlighting a perceived failure in themselves. So there is a need to blame someone else rather than become content with

THE SPIRIT OF CAIN

their current place or progress. Or they need to blame others if they have genuinely not progressed like they needed to, so they don't feel bad about themselves.

Cain will try to disqualify or discredit another's successes, or it will try to remove the person or steal their position or credit. Where I come from in New Zealand, they call this "tall-poppy syndrome." This is a society-based mindset in which there is almost a socialistic level of growth or standing. And if anyone exceeds or excels that level, people around that person will cut them down to size because another's success is a threat to them, or it is intimidating to the rest who are decidedly mediocre. The "cut down" can be *sincere* and *caring* in appearance, but the agenda is not in their best interest.

Cain doesn't really discuss his heart condition with Abel, for that would only serve to show weakness. This spirit of evil competition is pent up and compounds into something far more severe inside the individual. In an aggressive and competitive spirit, the person will never want to give up any perceived moral high ground so it will refuse true intimate accountability.

God has revealed to me how this spirit will harbor in a person who avoids true relational intimacy. Where fear obstructs a heartfelt relationship, this spirit will gain the advantage. Cain will always try and look like an innocent bystander during or after it has attempted to assassinate or destroy his competition.

In Genesis 4, we can see Cain's brazen face responding to God with no conviction when God came to him once again: "Then the LORD said to Cain, 'Where is Abel your brother?' He said, 'I do not know. Am I my brother's keeper?' And He said, 'What have you done? The voice of your brother's blood cries

THE SPIRIT OF CAIN

out to Me from the ground'" (Genesis 4:9–10). Cain's competition for God's approval had transformed into murderous hatred toward Abel, who had done right before God by bringing Him an offering from his flock. Abel's blood was now crying out from the ground for justice.

Abel didn't see Cain coming; otherwise, he would have tried to defend himself. And, dare I say it, many people or pastors don't see the spirit of Cain coming, while it is lurking in the shadows of their lives. Jacob, like Cain before him, also tried to hustle and get a desired result the easy way, trying to gain something quickly. The spirit of Cain will trample others out, taking the shortcut toward its goal. The fact remains, however, that we actually are our brother's and sister's keeper.

I have a dear friend who is doctor in psychiatry, and she once told me when discussing a sad situation we had both witnessed, that a psychopath is described as a person who is prepared to hurt and devastate others with the full understanding of the effect they are having on the lives of the people they harm. The harm they brought to others is done with an awareness of their own intentions and having a clear agenda in mind. No one else matters to them. It is easy to see the similarity of characteristics between the spirit of Cain and psychopathic tendencies. Cain's attitude says, "If I can't have or take what you have, then you shouldn't have it. So, therefore, I am going to ensure that you are demoted or dislodged so I can have what I see as rightfully mine."

Have you ever been promoted in a role at your job and felt others resented you out of jealously because you got what they wanted? This is just the tip of the iceberg in the DNA of

THE SPIRIT OF CAIN

humanity. And the spirit of Cain is not relegated to the corners of the church. This spirit operates in the world too. In fact, there is no corner of society it does not reach. Since the time of Adam, the spirit of Cain has plagued humanity with inherently destructive traits.

Two brothers, Adolf and Rudolph Dassler, during World War II, decided to get into the shoe business with one another. Rudolph (Rudi), being the exuberant salesman, and Adolph (Adi) was behind the scenes crafting these amazing shoes. Even though the brothers joined the Nazi party in 1933, the year Hitler took control, they were able to get Olympians to show off their product, and the result was that sales boomed.

Family strains developed during the Allied bomb attack on Herzogenaurach in 1943, however. As far as everyone knows, Adi and Rudi's wives did not get along. When Adi and his wife went into a bomb shelter for protection, they discovered Rudi and his family beat them to it. When Adi made a comment about the Allied warplanes, he blurted out, "The dirty bastards are back again." Rudolph became offended because he thought this remark was directed toward him. Nobody ever set things right, so there was never any restoration between the two brothers.

Adi started the business back up after the war by making shoes for the American GIs. When Rudi was called to serve at the front lines, he abandoned his post because he was convinced that Adi sent him there. Rudi was sent to prison for leaving his post. During the family feud, Adi worked on getting public exposure for his company, Adidas. While Rudi was always a few steps behind, he changed his company name from Ruda to Puma to sound more athletic. Even in their hometown, people

THE SPIRIT OF CAIN

who supported Adidas did not do business with people who were involved with Puma, and vice versa.

The competition between them ruined the chances for either one of them to be the top athletic shoe company, because the rivalry distracted them from their real competitive threat—Nike, who ended up taking the business lead. The two brothers died four years apart from each other and are buried in the same cemetery, their bodies being located on opposites sides of the graveyard. This spirit being present will ultimately end in division, character assassination, or, in extreme cases, even murder.

If you look at another aspect of World War II in Nazi Germany, one of the primary reasons the Jews were hated was because they were good business people and stewards of finances in the midst of a drastically financially depressed economy. They were a people who had many resources when a lot of people had nothing at all. Jealousy began to become the stimulus of antisemitism in the early period of Adolf Hitler's reign.

The Abrahamic blessing on the Jewish people manifested itself in the form of the material blessing they walked in. And the people became resentful of the Jewish residence in Germany. The resentment within the Nazi and Gestapo high command evolved into something in common with Cain, a "final solution" to eradicate the Jewish people. Slowly but surely Jewish citizens were herded like cattle in trains to death camps. It was easy for the Nazis to hate the Jews in this period of time, just as Cain hated Abel because Abel had what Cain wanted—he could not change that, so he killed him.

Notice God's warning to Cain still stands as a solemn warning to all sons and daughters of God today, even to all of humanity,

THE SPIRIT OF CAIN

who may feel provoked or have already begun to allow evil competition into their hearts: "Sin crouches at your door, but you must master it." Sin is always crouching at our door; the devil is an opportunist, waiting for the perfect time to strike. After tempting Jesus in the desert, the Bible records that the devil left and waited for a more opportune time to come back and tempt Him. Guard yourself from the spirit of Cain.

Chapter 4

THE STORY OF JACOB AND HIS DESCENDANTS

The story of Cain continues with the sons of Isaac—Jacob and Esau. It is the well-known story of two brothers who fought and contended, even in the womb, to be the firstborn, and then through the remainder of their lives they continued to fight. Jacob's competition with Esau brings perspective to the slow calculated competitor. The birthright and blessing were a point of contention and jealousy that Jacob, the supplanter and hustler, schemed over.

Although Jacob's story is mildly different to Cain's in the fact that he did not kill Esau, he did in fact take extreme advantage of his brother, to the point that he robbed him of his birthright. Jacob was opportunistic with Esau, coveting his birthright since he was old enough to understand what it was, learning that if he had been born first then he would be the rightful heir to all his father's inheritance. It most likely tormented Jacob, with thoughts of injustice and stolen entitlement. Over time, however, this most likely evolved into a strong disdain of Esau.

Like Cain and Abel, Jacob and Esau were two very different people. Esau was the rugged, manly hunter, and Jacob was more of a stay-at-home thinker who liked to cook. Esau was likely a rugged brute who excelled in all his hunter-gatherer qualities, a man who lived in the now, while Jacob was more of an intellect who thought ahead and slowly but surely carried out his plans and schemes.

We know that Esau despised and undervalued his birthright, and obviously Jacob valued it so much that he would do anything to get it. God later noted that He loved Jacob and hated Esau for these very reasons (Malachi 1:2–3). But I am focusing here on what was done, not what each of the two valued or devalued. It's great that Jacob valued the blessing, but I want to focus our attention on the competition that resided within Jacob's heart, causing him to run over his brother in order to get what he wanted.

The competition and jealousy that lay quietly in Jacob's heart, and that was later stimulated by his mother to further consolidate his feelings of injustice and entitlement, had a powerful effect on his and his brother's lives. Jacob swindled Esau out of the blessing that he had competed for before being born. He coveted the right thing, but he went about it in the wrong way. He lied to his

THE STORY OF JACOB AND HIS DESCENDANTS

own father, Isaac, who would have died knowing his son was a deceiver, seeming to be comfortable with the fact of deceiving his own dying father. I'm sure this must have tormented Isaac later in his life as he reflected on this incident.

Jacob would have no doubt heard the story of how there was a wresting for who was would be the firstborn while coming out of the womb. I have no understanding of what was actually taking place as unborn babies usually do not seem to have much capacity to scheme on that level—but it is clear that there was a striving going on even while Jacob and Esau were in their mother's womb. When our son was born, he was completely dependent on our care, along with the care the nurses gave, so it seems that this was either a complete mystery or a prophetic act that God allowed to happen.

Jacob's disdain must have grown for his brother as he watched him each day go about his life, walking in complete disregard for his birthright. This eventually caused Jacob to do something that had him fleeing for his life, while Esau woke up to the fact that Jacob robbed him of what was rightfully his. Just because Jacob was chosen by God and became the lineage through whom Christ came doesn't mean what he did was right in God's sight.

Esau must have been so enraged as he discovered that Jacob had not only swindled him that day when he traded lentil soup for his birthright, but years later Jacob had also secretly tricked their father while blind on his deathbed into believing that he was Esau coming to receive the blessing, securing the real estate of the inheritance that could be only given to the firstborn. The rage must have been so furious coming from Esau, who was known as the wild and rugged hunter, that Jacob's mother warned him to flee his brother's wrath and revenge. Jacob's mother told him to go and live with his uncle Laban, which Jacob did.

Jacob worked hard for Laban for years, but in the process he began to reap what he had sown. Laban had Jacob work for seven years to earn the hand of one his daughters in marriage, whom Jacob had fallen in love with. Except, on the wedding night, when Jacob was drunk, Laban switched out the daughter with his other daughter that the Bible says had dim eyesight. When Jacob woke up the next morning and saw that it was Leah, maybe Jacob then began to remember how he had treated people in his past as he felt the sting of being swindled himself.

Jacob worked for another seven years and eventually earned the right to marry Laban's daughter he had originally fallen in love with. He also struck an agreement with Laban that any sheep he shepherded that were born spotted or discolored would become his property, which was successful in that Jacob ended up becoming rich from many of the animals being born spotted and discolored. This must have bothered Laban, who in return felt swindled, but Jacob wasn't finished being a schemer. He took his two wives and all his flock and fled in the middle of the night, taking Laban's daughters far from his life.

It became evident that Jacob had a problem scamming everyone he met. Even though he understood and valued the blessing, that was no excuse for what he did to his own brother. We can never conclude that competing in such a way like Jacob, the trickster, can be acceptable—to swindle someone out of his or her position or possessions is never right. We will always reap what we have sown.

Jacob, fleeing Laban, then approached the land in which he

THE STORY OF JACOB AND HIS DESCENDANTS

grew up, and another facet of his past was now in front of him as he came to a river, on which the other side was his brother. Would Esau want to kill him for stealing his birthright from all those years prior? Or had Esau forgiven him for all the wrong Jacob had done to him? Whatever the case, Jacob was not so sure, and he was not going to be the first to find out.

He sent his family ahead of him across the river and waited in a place called Peniel, waiting to hear word that it was safe for him to cross over and meet Esau. The Word of God tells us about Jacob's Peniel experience, where he finally encountered the angel of the Lord, which many believe to be God Himself, and physically wrestled with Him till dawn. This wrestling with God caused Jacob to be changed forever; his name no longer being Jacob but Israel. Jacob had finally, after a lifetime of trickery, met someone he could not gain advantage over. His trickery, competition, deception, and taking things had finally been addressed by this encounter with God.

This is the spirit of Cain at work, the spirit that inflicts great damage and cuts divisions that last decades and lifetimes. This was true for Jacob—he got what he wanted but suffered as a result—and it is also true for us as well. Jacob's life reaped certain consequences as a result of this spirit at work in his heart. I'm sure his relationship with Esau was forever changed as a result, although some reconciliation did take place toward the end. We must learn from his life so that this too does not become our story.

The story of the spirit of Cain affecting the life of the people of God doesn't stop with Jacob, however. It continues with how Jacob's sons treated Joseph, their father's favored son. As we read in Genesis 37, we see that Israel was living in the land in which he journeyed with his wives and twelve sons. Joseph was his second youngest son, the son Israel favored above the other brothers because he was born later in his life. Because Benjamin and Joseph were sons of his wife Rachel, they held a special place in his heart.

Israel loved Joseph so much that he had a special and notable coat made for him—a cloak of many colors. All the other brothers had plain single-colored coats, and yet Joseph was dressed in brightly colored distinguished clothing. During that time, brightly colored clothing was a sign of nobility. This was not an issue of different-colored clothing like we would think of today in our modern world; rather, it was a status symbol.

Reuben, Israel's firstborn son, most likely felt that he deserved the honor of a multicolored coat, given that he had the birthright inheritance as was the way of his forefathers. But we read about Joseph sporting his bright coat in front of his brothers. He knows that the favor of his father is on him. And so do his brothers. Because of this favor, it sets in motion many painful events in Joseph's life. Joseph had a couple prophetic dreams from God in which it was indicated that he would be promoted and his brothers and parents would eventually bow down to him. Needless to say, the tension rose to a boiling point when he shared these dreams with his brothers and then with his father.

This is a great lesson for everyone to learn from, because God has special blessings—a calling and a destiny—for each and every person. All we need to do to receive it is hear what God is saying to us personally and to be obedient to what He tells us. In a moment, God can show us favor and even promise of promotion,

THE STORY OF JACOB AND HIS DESCENDANTS

but we must not gloat in it by boasting to our peers, or anyone for that matter. Gloating, boasting, or foolish announcements can stimulate competition like no other catalyst can. I was told early in my walk with the Lord to be careful about whom I shared my dreams with, "because people may not celebrate with you the way you think."

Here we see a young Joseph who lacked wisdom and in some ways may have been so innocent, even naïve, to the true nature of what jealousy could do in the hearts of humanity. But Solomon reminds us in Proverbs that discretion will keep us in all our ways (Proverbs 2:11), and I think it would be fair to say that Joseph was not necessarily wise or discrete in the way he announced the promise of God's favor on his life.

There is no doubt the seeds of jealousy and competition for their father's blessing, favor, and approval were planted in his brothers' hearts, surely growing after watching Joseph display his father's favor over the other eleven brothers each day as he proudly wore his coat. These dreams only fertilized the growing bitterness and resentment that was already deep within their hearts.

The same spirit of Cain we read about in Genesis 4 we can now see taking hold of his brothers' hearts in Genesis 37:11. After Joseph told them his dream, the Bible says, "And his brothers envied him, but his father kept the matter in mind." And the Word of God tells us later in the New Testament that "where envy and self-seeking exist, confusion and every evil thing are there" (James 3:16). In the case of Joseph, there was most definitely envy and tension present, which almost led to murder but settled instead in treachery, rejection, and betrayal.

His brothers were out tending their father's flock day after day while Joseph, the favored son, was living the high life under the shade of his father's tents at home. Israel asked Joseph to go out and check in on things, to see how his brothers were doing and how the flocks were doing. The favored but younger son was being sent out to oversee the older but more experienced, harder-working, and underappreciated brothers. He had already told them that he would rule over them one day, and now he was beginning to do that, though on a small level.

Like Cain, the sin that was crouching at his brothers' doors had already been let inside the house, making it easy to conspire and plot against Joseph. The ten older brothers would finally be free of their arrogant, boastful, favored younger brother. They could now eliminate the mountain between their underappreciated state and the favor of their father, which they coveted. All the ingredients were present for the spirit of Cain to be set in motion. And it is precisely here that we find Joseph thrown into the bottom of a pit at the angry and raging hands of his brothers.

You see, when the offense and resentment of jealousy and envy is fully rooted in a person, all that is lacking for sin to be expressed is an opportunity. This spirit is predatory in nature, but it waits for the perfect moment of vulnerability and privacy in which others will not be present or have privy to witness the assassination about to happen. This is the same way Cain killed Abel out in the field, not in front of Adam or Eve.

When his brothers threw Joseph into the pit, I am sure Joseph went from being on an assigned task by his father to instantly terrified for his very life. Unlike Abel before him, Joseph did not

THE STORY OF JACOB AND HIS DESCENDANTS

instantly die; rather, he had a revelation of just how far envy, jealousy, and competition had driven his brothers. He understood just how far the hate had caused his brothers to stoop in their morals. The Bible tells us:

> Now when they saw him afar off, even before he came near them, they conspired against him to kill him. Then they said to one another, "Look, this dreamer is coming! Come therefore, let us now kill him and cast him into some pit; and we shall say, 'Some wild beast has devoured him.' We shall see what will become of his dreams!"
> —GENESIS 37:18–20

Instead of Joseph's brothers killing him, however, we read that Reuben convinced the others not to kill him but instead to cast him into a pit. Joseph was completely helpless in the arms of his jealous brothers. His fate was now seemingly at their discretion: "So it came to pass, when Joseph had come to his brothers, that they stripped Joseph of his tunic, the tunic of many colors that was on him. Then they took him and cast him into a pit. And the pit was empty; there was no water in it" (Genesis 37:23–24).

The first thing that the brothers did was strip Joseph of his coat, which represented his father's honor. The spirit of Cain despises the blessing that comes into our lives. Each of these brothers were angry and had fallen countenances, just like Cain before them. They must have desired that robe—not because it was pretty material or regal in nature, but because only their father could authentically put the symbol of his honor on them. This is why the first thing they did was strip Joseph of his honor.

THE SPIRIT OF CAIN

Joseph's brothers then sat down to eat, obviously satisfied with themselves having just put Joseph into a prison of sorts. As they looked up from their food, they saw a company of the descendants of their grandfather's son, Ishmael, coming along. These were traders who were carrying spices and precious things bound for Egypt. They immediately began to rethink their scheme—now they would make profit from this treachery; now they would sell him. They traded Joseph for twenty shekels of silver, sold for money just like Jesus would be thousands of years later; Joseph was sold to a people who despised the descendants of Isaac.

As Joseph was led away behind the caravan of camels, disappearing into the sea of sand heading toward Egypt, his brothers turned to each other and began to plan how they could be absolved of responsibility to their father. They planned how they could look innocent after such vicious treachery, which is a consistent trait of someone operating in the spirit of Cain—there is almost a split personality in the condition. There is a deep-seated hatred toward an individual, and so the person allows himself or herself to come into agreement with the spirit of Cain. And yet there is still a fundamental value of the blessing, so there is a switch of masks once the deed is done. They go from being jealous and murderous, dissociation with the act of treachery, back toward an appearance of innocence that pretends to know nothing of what has been done.

The brothers took Joseph's robe and, like crooked police officers, began to plan their alibi:

> So they took Joseph's tunic, killed a kid of their flock of goats, and dipped the tunic in the blood. Then they

THE STORY OF JACOB AND HIS DESCENDANTS

sent the tunic of many colors, and they brought it to their father and said, "We have found this. Do you know whether it is your son's tunic or not?" And he recognized it and said, "It is my son's tunic. A wild beast has devoured him. Without doubt Joseph is torn to pieces."

—GENESIS 37:31–33

Joseph's brothers claimed to know nothing about the sin they had just carried out. The cloak was then taken back to Israel, who in the moment recognized it as the coat his son Joseph used to wear. Israel probably didn't realize that he was reaping a harvest from the same spirit of Cain he had operated in against his brother, Esau, years earlier, and also the same spirit he operated in when deceiving his father, Isaac.

Joseph's journey was altered in a traumatic way—a son with so much favor tragically sold into slavery. However, we know that God worked all things together for good and used all of the horrible circumstances surrounding Joseph's life to save the people of Israel—his father and brothers and decedents. In fact, we know that he went on to help save the lands surrounding the whole region as he wisely governed under Pharaoh. Joseph's story ended well, but do not underestimate the evil that took place within his siblings' relationships, which was all motivated by envy and jealousy—the spirit of Cain.

Chapter 5

A THREATENED KING

In the story of Saul and David, we see yet another application of the spirit of Cain at work. But this time it is not someone longing for a greater position than what they already have—it is someone who is jealous of a person under him or her. The already-anointed-and-appointed-favored king, Saul, is threatened by the favor of another man after God's own heart—David. In this case, as far as position is concerned, we see the greater man hunt the lesser, attempting to murder him. The stunning point of difference here is that we see that Cain operates both upward and downward when it comes to favor and position.

The first time Saul met David was in Saul's tent overlooking the battlefield, as Goliath the giant roared intimidating threats and taunts at the army of Israel. This relationship that began in celebration would escalate into a jealous rage that sparked one of Israel's most well-known manhunts. When they first met, the king embraced David as the only son of Israel who had courage to stand up to the giant. In this case, Saul was more than happy for David to be the better man and to volunteer to fight the giant.

Saul embraced David as a courageous hero that day. The events that followed, in which, gripped by the Spirit of God, David would defy and slay Goliath, the champion of the Philistine camp, one of the giant sons of Anakin, would be another story entirely. That day David was a hero to all of Israel, and rightly so—he had slain the giant who was taunting the armies of Israel. But there was something about David that Saul did not know. David was sovereignly and secretly anointed king by Samuel before Saul even knew who David was—he was the one who was selected by God as the next to sit on the throne. Not only was he going to be the next king, but David was the one who was selected to be the figurehead in the lineage of Jesus.

David became the champion of Israel after defeating Goliath, and his fame spread throughout the land. Of course they didn't have mass media in that day to share their stories; instead, the stories and eyewitness accounts of his victories and conquests would have been heard throughout the city daily and become a common topic among the people. David's fame had spread through the land so much as he started having victory after victory. The Lord was with David, and as the years went by he carried out many victories over the enemy in battle. His name was becoming more and more renowned, so the people sang in

A THREATENED KING

the streets, "Saul has slain his thousands, and David his ten thousands" (1 Samuel 18:7).

Upon hearing this, Saul's heart began to experience anxiety at the thought that someone else was possibly better than him, or more highly esteemed by the people than he was. After all, some of Saul's greatest mistakes were centered on trying to look great in the eyes of Israel. This means he obviously coveted in his heart the fame and praise of the people. The fury began to kindle in Saul's heart toward the young David, who was daily growing in favor with all the people.

As time went on, these chants began to torment Saul. The competition and jealousy that was already within him was beginning to boil over. Instead of standing securely in his office as the king of all Israel, he began to feel threatened by someone else who was doing well. Instead of supporting and championing David, like he had previously done in his defeat of Goliath, Saul was now provoked in his own rivalry and envy with David's achievements and growing celebrity that he began to entertain murderous thoughts toward him.

Saul was mentally tormented and his thoughts became consumed with murder. This was directed toward the very same young man who had played the harp to the Lord in Saul's court and set him free of the tormenting demon spirit. Saul was chosen to be the king of Israel, and Samuel anointed him as the people refused God as their King. They wanted to be like the other nations around them, so they demanded a king.

Saul was a good-looking man with a tall and handsome stature; he was regal and macho, given his description in the book of Samuel. Being Israel's first king, Saul had been used to being

THE SPIRIT OF CAIN

adored by the people and looked to as the pinnacle of Israel. But now the attention that he had grown to love was being taken away from him and was starting to shine on another. That called into question his humanity and kingship—the very fabric of the celebrity that Saul loved about himself was now in the shadows of David's notoriety that was building as each day passed.

Saul's entire identity had become consumed with his role as king. And he became so childish in his approach and heart condition that no one else could be great and detract from his apparent greatness. This came to the point where he was so threatened by the success of another that he would set himself against anyone else who would be seen to shine brighter. The seed of Cain was now lodged well inside Saul's being. Because Saul's heart was prejudiced toward David, his heart became hard.

It is easy for people to see this spirit of Cain in a situation in which Abel does right and is accepted, and then Cain, the rejected, becomes jealous and strikes out. They see Abel as the one in position and Cain not in a position of power. But here we see Saul in the position of power—not David, even though he was anointed for the throne. Saul is the one striking at David, not the other way around. Saul's heart was so deranged with jealousy and competition, and he was so possessed by the spirit of Cain, that a king who should be noble and regal became a psychotic who attempted murder multiple times.

Saul tried to personally kill David at least two times, as well as many other times using his army. When instructed to destroy all of the Amalekites, he preserved some animals and King Agag, and yet he made it his life's obsession to try and destroy David's life. And just like Cain, Saul tried to offer a sacrifice before the Lord that was unacceptable as Samuel walked onto the battlefield.

David's anointing to be king must have tormented Saul from the perspective of feeling threatened, but it was jealousy, envy, and competition that were mostly at work within his heart. In order to thrive in or through an individual, the spirit of Cain requires insecurity, and Saul most definitely fitted the profile. Saul, a seasoned warrior himself, tried to kill David by throwing a javelin at him in the courtroom. Since Saul was a warrior himself, he knew how to throw the javelin—he had probably killed many men before with it.

Jealousy drove Saul toward a murderous manhunt. His desire was to make David such an outlaw that his fame would become forgotten and he would never be able to ascend the throne. But I would speculate that Saul never told his advisors and captains of the army that he was jealous—as the spirit of Cain will rarely admit jealousy. Instead, he proceeded to create reasons that were explainable excuses to pursue David the way he did. Saul understood that if he could murder the elusive David then he could destroy his character and credibility.

Cain is a murderous spirit and will manifest murder either in the natural, spoken, or emotional realm. We know that David was so stealthy that he had Saul in a vulnerable moment in which he was planning to kill him, but the Lord stayed David's hand and he only took a piece of Saul's robe. David was close enough to God and mature enough in spiritual wisdom to not retaliate on Saul in the same manner that Saul pursued him. David was wise enough to run to safety and stay humble during this time.

Brother David Hogan, who has been a missionary in Mexico

THE SPIRIT OF CAIN

for forty years, has been a great hero in the faith to me since my late teens, when I first heard him speak and operate in the power of God like the disciples in the book of Acts. And I have been blessed to have a relationship with him and have him speak into my life in recent years as a mentor. When walking through a very difficult period of life, experiencing things that should not happen in the church but sadly do, Brother David gave me counsel to remember David in the book of Samuel.

When a nation was captured or beaten in battle, the king of that nation was usually killed in conquest to destroy the morale of the conquered nation. The Philistines would have put Saul to death if David had not fought Goliath, which means that Saul owed his life to David. And yet Saul hunted David, trying to murder him, all because of jealousy.

David and his mighty men had returned after they had been out fighting only to discover their women and children had been taken. Because of what took place, David's own men began to turn on him and blame him for what took place. Ironically, these were all the men who should have been forever grateful to him for their very lives. These were his own men he had strengthened and built up in the cave of Adullam, to the point that they became mighty men of valor.

David had the right to retaliate out of sheer frustration; instead, however, he took off his armor and worshiped in his ephod before the Lord. He was completely vulnerable before God. The greatest response when being attacked by a spirit of Cain is to be vulnerable in worshiping before the Lord. Let God be your defender and vindicator. David responding to Saul would have made David just as bad as Saul—but unlike Saul, David turned his heart to worship the Lord. Brother David Hogan encouraged me, at a time in my life when I had every right in the natural to respond to a Saul, to take the low place, worship God, and allow Him to fight my battles for me.

In my twenties and early thirties, I served a traveling minister on numerous ministry trips to many churches all over the world. I was not on staff or paid by this minister, mostly paying my own airfares and donating my own time to go and serve him as an armor bearer—it cost me a great deal in time and travel expenses. I valued being around what God was doing as a joy, not resenting the cost.

The man carries a great anointing and has been a blessing to many people and places, but I would be shocked because he would often discredit other traveling ministers and preachers to the local pastors. I would watch him compete against other ministers as he genuinely thought he was better than each of them, a more anointed individual. I would even watch as he would compete against the local pastors in front of their churches he would be preaching at. Furthermore, he would make statements to some of these ministers, alluding to the fact that I was his personal assistant and that he paid me, instead of just honestly saying that I was his friend who had personally paid to come along and serve. I don't know how many people saw through it, but I surely did. There were massive levels of insecurity that fueled competition in him not just to be noticed but also to elevate and compare himself against other ministers. There was an aggressive push to get to the top and become noticed with the perception of success, not really considering who was getting hurt or run over in the process. It is amazing how people become actors to get what they want, all the while suppressing

THE SPIRIT OF CAIN

and harboring a secret agenda and sentiment of aggression toward those around them they are quietly competing against.

We must always remember that ministering is to serve, not to be seen or served. The spirit of Cain will always seek to promote itself and then pursue those who are in a lesser position if it feels threatened by other perceived potential rivals. It is always fighting to get to the top or prevent others from being promoted or seen as equal or superior. We must be free from this spirit in our lives.

I attended church in my twenties alongside a young man I had been privileged to lead to the Lord. We were both called by God to serve in full-time ministry. At first there was some levels of unbalanced youthful zeal present in us as we grew in God, which is normal for most new believers. But it wasn't long before I started picking up on an extreme competitive spirit present within this young man toward myself and others. The Holy Spirit taught me a great deal through this season of my life; it is not easy when you feel envy and competition constantly dishonoring you.

Have you ever been chased by a dog while you rode your bike down the street? The dog is actually fixated with the spinning of the wheels and seems to get totally mesmerized by them. It is usually not after you per se, but after the spinning of the wheel. The evil competition that resides in a person's heart is much the same—people get totally fixated on the competitive nature and are jealous of all kinds of things. After a while it's like the dog chasing the bike wheels—the very reason it began can't be recalled because they have lost themselves in a rivalry that has them completely consumed.

It was not long before this young man began to make

declarations to myself and in small groups that he was praying that he would know the Word of God better than each of us. His desire to know God's Word wasn't bad in and of itself, but benchmarking and condescending to other people that his agenda was to be better than everyone else certainly started to communicate loud and clear the unhealthy competition present in his heart.

He ended up becoming so consumed with competition and rivalry over the years that it caused our relationship to distance. The reality is that you cannot walk closely with someone who is not genuinely for you and does not authentically celebrate you. Unfortunately, the spirit of Cain manifested in many different forms over the next decade. There were moments when I was honored or promoted, and I would be congratulated through "gritted teeth," but all the while I would feel his disdain disqualifying me in his mind.

He had grown up in a large family and was often overlooked at certain times, while at other times he would need to compete for attention—this grew unchecked in his spiritual DNA as he progressed in the Christian faith. It started off with little things, but it slowly grew over the years. In fact, early on the Holy Spirit warned me that the relationship would be like Cain and Abel. The Lord began to reveal to me the root issue about the spirit of Cain—this is where He first began to teach me about the spirit of Cain and evil competition.

I learned to keep a good heart through that period of my life, celebrating as the Lord would prepare a table before me even when those around me were not for me. The truth is that this young man and I were supposed to work together building the kingdom of God, but like Paul said on one occasion, "Then the contention became so sharp that they parted from one another. And so Barnabas took Mark and sailed to Cyprus" (Acts 15:39).

There are certain times in life when love does not require us to continue in a contentious or harmful relationship or situation. In Paul's case, he decided that for his own good he would go separate ways from Barnabas. The point is that God desires us to be fruitful and productive with our lives. When individuals become so abrasive over long periods of time with no sign of restoration or repentance, it can be wise to consider going separate ways in order to protect yourself from being distracted from the ultimate task of God's will for your life.

The Word of God instructs us that "if it is possible, as much as depends on you, live peaceably with all men" (Romans 12:18). The plain truth is that this indicates that it is not an absolute to live peaceably with everyone, so in some cases it is wiser to move forward on the direction God has for us, rather than continuing in an unhealthy environment or relationship.

My relationship with this man was marked by constant critical character assassination of others and myself over the years; sometimes it was difficult as this constant hounding of competition where I would be falsely accused or critiqued would be humiliating and hurtful. I never brought it up with my pastor, whom I was close with, something I could have easily done. Rather, I kept it to myself and trusted God to vindicate me. This man looked for even the slightest chink or crack in my armor to point the finger at, somehow seeking to devalue and demote me in an unspoken rivalry. This never really bothered me, however, as I refused to reciprocate in this hidden power struggle for position or affirmation, it was my nonresponse that kept me safe.

A THREATENED KING

The worst thing any of us can do is agree to engage in this unhealthy competition and enter into an ungodly two-way rivalry. None of us are perfect and every relationship needs grace, no matter how spiritual, mature, or holy the individual may appear. But Cain takes no prisoners; it does not look through the eyes of grace. Rather, it looks across the battlefield like a general strategizing on how to defeat the opponent. It studies the strengths and weaknesses of the enemy and waits for the perfect opportunity, which will often have a shock and awe characteristic to it.

The element of surprise is the most valuable strategy to any military force—it was valuable to Cain when he murdered Abel. Later, in a vulnerable moment in which I was helping this young man, he mentioned that he had always felt threatened by me in his mind, and he realized there was no need to. He admitted that he had always tried to be like me. It was then that I began to see exactly what God had been telling me years earlier was far more accurate than I first realized.

When this unhealthy competition and jealousy are present in our lives, there will be gross overcompensations in behavior and actions so that people are validated or noticed. Sometimes, these become so aggressively strong that they become offensive or hurtful to the very people being competed against. This is not just a sinful characteristic of human nature, although human nature is involved; rather, it is the influence of a demon spirit.

Unfortunately, when wounds are present and unhealthy competition is part of a person's mind-set, if the spirit of Cain is present you will need to understand that the devil may have found a vehicle to use to carry out this evil strategy. However, the good news is that Jesus is King and He defeated the devil, sin, and death! This means that, through Jesus' death on the cross and His bodily resurrection, He defeated the spirit of Cain on your behalf. If this spirit is currently operating in a person around you, God will give you a strategy to navigate around it and outwit the enemy's plan. While you are engaging the spirit of Cain, it is important to remember that you are not wrestling against flesh and blood but against demonic forces of wickedness.

The devil tries to set brother against brother and friend against friend, but he does not wait until people are in their teenage years to introduce this spirit. Rather, he starts early, often in childhood and home environments. The devil understands that if he can sow the seed of this evil characteristic into our formative years, then he will have a foothold and something to work with later in life. The devil is and always has been in the business of attempting to destroy lives. Therefore, we must be wise to this fact and understand his strategies and sidestep his snares.

Have you ever seen children competing or fighting with their siblings for their parents' affection or approval? It's an instinctive nature to desire to be loved and affirmed by parents. But it is in our fallen sinful nature that then sees other children as a threat to our parents' love of us. How about trying to run faster than your sibling or perform better than he or she did at a certain activity? You weren't trying to be the best, but to be approved more highly.

This mind-set then compounds into a lifelong trait of unspoken competition between siblings, which is then transferred onto friends and peers later in life. The spirit of Cain causes an unspoken benchmark to be set by other siblings and people where the other person's progress or achievement becomes the mark to beat. The individual becomes the target of a powerful and driven ambition to succeed in what they have done or have, or at times make them feel like this is a truly horrible experience. This can breed mistrust between siblings and people in such a way that an individual will not receive any advice, caring, loving correction, or warnings from another because they have a mind-set where the other person is almost in the enemy category and cannot be trusted because they actually might be trying to sabotage their destiny or potential success.

Competition is rooted and founded by pride. And pride will always defend dysfunction. Therefore, competition rooted in rejection, insecurity, and pride will not allow you to excel into the true blessing of God; it will rob you of the best God has for you, trying to steal your peace. It has a quiet but strong disdain toward other perceived opponents, and all of their weaknesses and flaws are studied and noted for the purpose of maneuvering into higher positions in the eyes of a father or mother, or other various leadership figures.

I used to box when I was younger. Before a fight I would study the abilities and weaknesses of the opponent. In sports, this is acceptable, but not so in relationships or within the kingdom of God. This present world sees this kind of treacherous behavior in the corporate world as normal and to be expected in the climb up the corporate ladder, thinking nothing of character assassination and trampling underfoot and climbing over the ruins of opponents' lives in order to grasp the crown and position of the apex leader. This evil culture is the way of Cain and is not acceptable in the kingdom of God.

Remember what Jesus said to Peter: "If you live by the sword,

THE SPIRIT OF CAIN

you will die by the sword" (Matthew 26:52). In addition to this, expounding on the advice to Peter that if you operate in evil competition and character assassination to claw and scratch your way into greater position in the kingdom, the same spirit will consume you—what you sow you will surely reap. This is common among ambitious young people who are on fire for the kingdom of God and who are full of zeal but lack wisdom in this matter.

We must realize that promotion does not come from the east or from the west; it comes from the Lord. Manipulating the circumstances or eliminating the competition does not bring true promotion into our lives, though we may be promoted for a short time. But in the end, it will end in an implosion and consuming of a backlash of this spirit on the one operating in it.

Think of it this way. Jesus said, "I am the way, the truth, and the life" (John 14:6). This means that He is the gateway to the kingdom, and everyone trying to enter any other way is a thief and a robber. Jesus represented and lived in everything that was opposite to evil competition—He lived in total submission and partnership with the Father. As a result of living with this Godward focus, He was promoted.

This teaches us to always take the low road in all of our relationships. Humility is attractive to God—there is great safety in it. Self-promotion, strife, wars, and division are earthly and sensual...and far below your heavenly call. Paul reminded the Corinthians of this very fact:

> And I, brethren, could not speak to you as to spiritual people but as to carnal, as to babes in Christ. I fed you

A THREATENED KING

> with milk and not with solid food; for until now you were not able to receive it, and even now you are still not able; for you are still carnal. For where there are envy, strife, and divisions among you, are you not carnal and behaving like mere men? For when one says, "I am of Paul," and another, "I am of Apollos," are you not carnal?
>
> —1 Corinthians 3:3–4

It is tragic how the devil has taken a perfectly good desire to be loved and distorted it to be something to fight over. We must counter his schemes using wisdom and love that come from above.

The Bible says, "Hell is bound up in the heart of a child but discipline will drive it from them" (Proverbs 22:15). Parents, we must disciple and teach our children to never compete against each other for our love, approval, or attention. There is enough love and approval for each child to securely walk through life being approved and full of identity. If we can counter this subtle culture, then we can help the next generation realize that each of us can walk before God in the same way—under the absolute approval, love, and attention of God. We can all walk in our individual callings, secure in our unique gifts and identity. There's enough love, promotion, and positions to go around for everyone in the kingdom if we just start looking at God and stop comparing ourselves with each other.

In some homes, parents have created a competitive environment in which siblings compete against each other for everything—even love, affection, and worth. If this is your story, then you must go to God the Father and seek healing. You must ask Him to show you His heart and His love toward you. You need to ask Him to transform your perspective of the Kingdom so that you can truly grasp how unhealthy competitiveness is not His way of doing things.

When I was young in God, a lot of zealous and on-fire young men and women who strongly felt called by the Lord surrounded me. Even though I was part of a church during this time, in many ways it felt like a Bible college environment. It was a testing environment, one that immunized me from this spirit of competition as I became repulsed by the constant jostling for position and being noticed as the most spiritual by the lead pastor. This was never discouraged; so in many ways it was encouraged.

The church is not like a sports team; individuals are not to be set against each other for better results. There is no good end to this strategy—it is only a twisted concept. There would be fierce unspoken competition from individuals who were hungry and would stop at nothing to attain recognition and position. People would be slandered and strategically reported on with an intent to disqualify their promotion or recognition. If someone was being considered to preach or minister on any level, there were instances of others bringing up issues and twisting the truth in order to cancel the plans of another being given the opportunity. Or after someone would speak, they would be critiqued to the point of looking like a failure—all in order to somehow promote themselves.

I led a home group at my house, along with many of the other young leaders at the time. Early on, I remember there was one young man who was so ambitious that he secretly talked to all of the stronger people in my group and convinced them to come to

A THREATENED KING

his group instead. This obviously benefited him on some level, causing him to look good in the short term. But in the long term, that competitive nature was unfortunately replicated into many people who followed him. Competition in this form is never fruitful for the good of the whole.

Character assassination toward you is not something that can ever be avoided; people are going to talk bad about you at some point in your life in some way or the other. You are going to be confronted with this, but God has not called you to live neutrally and politically correct so that no one ever has a bad thing to say about you. No, in fact, we are warned in the Word to beware when everyone is speaking well of us (Luke 6:26). The spirit of Cain will do all it can to assassinate your character. But you must respond like David did, with strengthening yourself in the Lord.

Chapter 6

THE MAKING OF A MUTINY

Absalom had a beautiful sister named Tamar. He also had a half brother named Amnon, who was also a son of the king and who had an unhealthy obsession with his half sister Tamar. Amnon became so infatuated with Tamar that he engineered circumstances in which he raped her and immediately afterward he rejected her and sent her away, thus bringing great shame on her. This naturally echoed shame and rage throughout the family, so Absalom began to seek to put right this terrible wrong of his sister's honor and virtue. He planned vengeance against Amnon, a justice of sorts, without the consent of his father, the king. Absalom assumed the role of judge and executioner, bypassing the king's approval. Like Cain

THE SPIRIT OF CAIN

living years before him, he waited for the conditions to be perfect in which he would strike and cut down the man who had wronged his sister.

Second Samuel 14:11 refers to the same thing in Cain's story, where the subject of "the avenger of blood" is raised. Just like Abel's blood crying out from the ground demanding justice, Cain will always demonstrate an injustice that was done. At this point David should have addressed the issues more directly in Absalom as his father, but rather it was almost smoothed over. Absalom was the favorite son of Israel, as far as his good looks went. He rode the favor of his good looks instead of developing discipline in his character.

Regarding favor, the problem with gifts and physical looks is that no one earns these things; rather, God gives them. A gift is not anything that can validate a person—they never paid the price to be good looking; they were born that way. They never created their gift by what they did; they are merely stewards of it. They cannot prove worth, but rather only stewardship of something that has been given to them.

Absalom burned down fields of crop to manipulate and used Joab to act as a go-between for himself and his father. In fact, he was insincere when he repented to his father. This is blatantly apparent because, immediately after David forgave him and accepted him, he began to divert honor away from his father by sitting at the city gates and competing for the throne by drawing all the people toward him.

There is a well-known spirit of Absalom, and I am not taking away from that; however, we can also see in this young man's story the spirit of Cain at work. What was it that caused him to rally together a mutiny against his father? We know the mutinous and treacherous spirit behind the rebellion that led a troop against King David to be the Absalom spirit, but where did it begin? What seeded this in Absalom, and how did it evolve?

I would like to suggest that the spirit of Absalom can look like the spirit of Cain with agreement and company. But don't confuse the spirit of Cain with the spirit of Absalom. Here are some ways I tell them apart. Cain operates mainly on its own, while Absalom requires a crowd. But Cain in many respects is the spirit that can lead into the more blatant expression of the spirit of Absalom. The spirit of Cain is brother rising against brother for base motives of jealousy, competition, and rivalry. The spirit of Absalom, on the other hand, always starts as the spirit of Cain internally and slowly turns the heart cold and venomous and commences to then build a mutinous gathering. The Absalom spirit looks more like Cain with an army. Cain is more of a singular spirit, whereas the Absalom spirit requires a group or crowd.

Looking back at Absalom's life, due to some of the things he did, he most likely felt that he was rejected and disqualified. Some of his actions caused an outcast mentality to be on his life, which probably contributed to a form of independence and insecurity. He probably considered that the throne was his right and his looks had achieved strong favor from the people, but due to his actions he was not favored or respected. However, entitlement gripped his heart and those psychological mind games consumed him daily.

If he considered the throne his right, then, David stood in the way of him being able to get it. But instead of trying to slay David

THE SPIRIT OF CAIN

in the field like Cain did with Abel, we know that Absalom "set up shop" down at the city gates and told the people something to the effect of, "Don't bother King David—my father is too busy—let me judge between you." His actions revealed a desire to do this for show, revealing that he was only jealous and competitive for the throne. The spirit of Absalom took over and he began to plot a rebellion and a mutiny against King David, eventually culminating in a small-scale war against him.

We can learn a great deal from Absalom's story from the eyes of the spirit of Cain. First, creating a loving environment is not enough to stop this evil competition from taking place. David was loving and overly gracious to Absalom, even when he should have dealt with his son's root issues in the moment that Absalom fell down before him. Because he did not deal with it right then and there, the spirit of competition and division began to war against King David in the form of a seed. The seed, when full grown, will act independently outside of godly authority, and begin to position itself to act in a way that is a reaction to a perceived but unreal injustice. This spirit must be exposed and taught with the fear of the Lord, along with a sound grasp of God's loving heart.

Second, Absalom took his time in setting up his mutiny against the king. He was down at the city gates gathering a loyal allegiance and following that he systematically plundered from the king's subjects for forty years (2 Samuel 15:1–7). This spirit always looks innocent at first appearances, and many times will drop subtle hints and not overt statements to reveal itself.

Absalom was a prince, not a king. But he stopped acting like a prince and became that of a rival king. There is vulnerability

THE MAKING OF A MUTINY

in love. We can see that God was to some degree vulnerable to betrayal in heaven and also with humans on the earth—so was David. But never mistake or become familiar with love and grace coming from God-ordained authority. Selfish ambition will see love as weakness, or it will look to exploit flaws and faults in leaders. Flaws and faults will always be found, for people are only human. But when evil competition is present within them, it will look to take advantage by character assassination, like Noah's son who thought nothing of mocking his father in a moment of vulnerability after leading the family in deliverance through one of the greatest disasters of all time by listening to God's voice.

This Absalomic competition lays in wait for an opportune time to sow division and offense, which is usually due to an unfulfilled expectation of promotion or power not being met. This entitlement mentality is a manifestation of pride and insecurity, which is why the writer of Hebrews warns us to look carefully "lest anyone fall short of the grace of God; lest any root of bitterness springing up cause trouble, and by this many become defiled" (Hebrews 12:15). The interesting part of Absalom is that a bitter root of offense rose up in his heart, causing him to defile anyone who would listen to him. And all who followed became enemies of David.

I witnessed a tragic church split in which two men in particular rallied against the leadership and seeded all kinds of accusations against them. It was extremely tragic as the long-term fallout and casualties were significant. It was apparent that these two men seemed to believe that they knew and could lead better than the people God had actually appointed to pastor the

THE SPIRIT OF CAIN

church. They struck at a vulnerable time and took a good number of people with them. These two men had a lust for power, and the sad thing is that they were actually called of God to be raised up but were not ready at that time to be promoted. They were apparently not happy with God's process—they wanted power and position now, so they created accusations in order to get to the place.

Competition will always strike, then try to look spiritual and innocent after it has caused destruction. Angels became demons in Lucifer's fall, and Absalom's troop became an army that was defeated by King David. Ultimately, all who are seduced by this spirit are in one of two groups of people: they are either naïve or they have seeds of the same offense and rebellion in their own hearts, as like spirits will always attract and congregate together.

This is why we must take into captivity every thought that rises up in our minds and hearts against the knowledge of Christ. The enemy must not be able to lodge a seed in our hearts for consideration. Leading or following this evil spirit of competition will always lead to destruction because it defies the God-ordained leadership that is set in place.

This story of Absalom's life and demise is the perfect introduction to understanding the demonic strategy found in church splits. Sadly, most Christians have experienced the effects of a church split in some form or another. And, again, while the Absalom spirit is also to blame for influencing splits, the spirit of Cain will seed and prelude the actual split. The spirit of Cain is always present before there is a split that occurs within a church.

Even though the enemy's camp is divided, it still somehow works together through fear in order to achieve objectives. There are different demons that march under different ranks and banners; for instance, there is a demon of hatred and a demon of unforgiveness. Each of these have functions, just as in God's kingdom there are warring angels and ministering angels. With that being said, it is important to understand that the spirit of Cain and the spirit of Absalom, although not the same spirit, do in fact work together.

The demon-possessed man Jesus delivered had multiple demons infesting his life and mind—the Bible calls it a "legion." If we can truly shed a Holy Spirit spotlight on this spirit, we will be able to uproot many inroads the enemy uses to birth division, schisms, and feuds in the beginning stages. Once the root of bitterness has found access and agreement through one mouth, inevitably, as the Word warns us, many will be defiled.

The spirit of Absalom is out to kill the sons and daughters of promise; it is out to ruin churches that are breaking and taking ground in the realm of the Spirit. If the devil can get his way into a church, many innocent young believers can be wounded for life in such a way that they may never fully trust leaders or church communities the same way again if healing doesn't occur.

The enemy is out to sabotage all the work the church does, the work that pastors have invested into building the kingdom of God in a local community, sometimes taking place over generations. One of his greatest strategies against the kingdom of God is a church split. The only thing more devastating than a local church split would be moral failure by someone in senior leadership.

The story of church splits almost always involves pride, ego, and power struggles centering around one or all of the concepts

THE SPIRIT OF CAIN

of injustice, conspiracy, or entitlement. In the initial stage of a church split scenario, the spirit of Cain takes action when an individual feels like they are entitled to more power or position than they are currently acknowledged as having. They begin to fester on the fact that they feel neglected or overlooked; some will even use that common word found in rebellion—they feel "controlled."

Prior to any outward expression or verbiage, however, the seeds of jealousy subtly take root in the person's mind. It may be someone who has a religious spirit and is so concerned about minute points of doctrine, or it may be a person who currently doesn't have a role and who feels they should have a position in the church or ministry. Or, even more boldly, sometimes the individual believes they should be the senior pastor; it can also be one of the other leaders in the church, like the youth pastor who begins to experience youthful pride in the progress or growth he has made.

Ultimately, any outward rebellion or mutiny is the spirit of Absalom, but the spirit of Cain is the instigator that provokes and torments the mind with jealousy and competition. This then motivates the person to commence down that dark trail of rebellion. Let's examine this with a case study.

Let's say that a young man, with no pastoral experience at all, is placed by pastoral leadership into a trusted role as youth pastor in a small church. There is an obvious call of God on his life. A little time passes, then suddenly he begins to see some growth and a few numbers being added to the youth group. This strokes his ego, so he begins to look over and compare his position to the senior pastor's role and the seed of competition is sown.

THE MAKING OF A MUTINY

Entitlement is now beginning to whisper in his ear, "You deserve a greater position. Look at what you're doing—these people love you and trust you." As he begins to think about this more and more, the thought comes, "You know how to do this better than the leaders who put you in this position." Pride begins to blind his senses and humility is fast leaving his heart. Slowly, whether consciously or unconsciously, a lack of gratitude for the trusted position he is in, along with jealousy and rivalry have been birthed in his heart.

This will remain there, silently growing below the surface, until it has reached a scale in which he becomes passive-aggressive toward the senior pastor or leadership team. As more time passes, he now has the desire to strike out in one form or another. While all this is happening, he most likely has no idea, still being relatively young, of just what it took to build the church from the ground up.

Cain has an entitlement mentality attached to it, with no real concept of the time it takes to earn or create something. It sees another's success or promotion and seeks to take it by force. Cain takes the ingrained, God-given human desire to be accepted and blessed and perverts it so that the individual looks to take it from their peers rather than become qualified for the blessing in the eyes of God. This is where the plan is forged in this young man's mind, in the midst of demonic pressure and torment that he is now in agreement with, losing all concept of spiritual reality. He is now intoxicated in his own proud, twisted perspective.

He will begin to relationally distance himself from the senior pastor like Absalom did for two years while living in the city without seeing David, which is where the spirit of Absalom has access. Once he begins to gather support and voice his perceived grievance with others around him, then Absalomic treachery and mutiny is present. This is where this spirit will use all of the offenses and bitterness that have grown through the spirit of Cain, where the young youth pastor never dealt with his heart and mastered his sin.

Unless a miracle occurs in this man's heart, the demonic assignment will gather as many people into this now festering conspiracy, poisoning their minds and hearts, distracting them from being focused on their love for God and each other. Now these people, who should have been protected by this young youth pastor in his trusted role, have been made victims of slander and mistrust, and they will begin to refuse to receive from their senior pastor the way they used to. Over time, the senior pastor has lost credibility and, in most cases, has been considered guilty until proven innocent. This happens because most people believe the first thing they hear and are emotionally led in their judgment.

The next step is that this young once pure-hearted youth pastor will decide that he can no longer stay at the church with so much "injustice" present. He will either conclude that he needs to help as many people leave as possible to escape the "spiritual abuse" that is taking place or the "lack of maturity or wisdom," whichever explanation he decides to believe, or he will take as many people as he can to start his own church and build his own throne.

In the heat of the moment, this youth pastor has no idea of the permanent damage his actions will inflict into innocent lives of the congregation over the years to come. They may not have the depth, maturity, or character to endure long-term upheaval. Initially, the people will look OK, but months and years later the true effects of such demonic division will begin to surface in their lives if not addressed and healed.

You can see in the above example that the spirit of Cain is operating with the intent to strike the delegated authority. Once the young man was put into a trusted pastoral role and tasted power, his desire was for more and more power. It became a lust for what he had not earned or qualified for, but rather for what another had. In the design of God, with obedience and diligence, he would eventually inherit promotion. Naturally, he began to look at the more established leadership all the while overvaluing his own input and in jealousy undervaluing and dishonoring his God-given covering and authority that put him in the role in the first place. This all happens because the young man now wants what the senior leaders have.

Jealousy and competition psychologically need a valid reason to be present, so criticisms and accusations are fabricated in the mind to make the rivalry somehow look like justice—and even a spiritual duty in some cases. We can see Cain operating not to the extent of murder but rather toward character assassination and eventual feuds. In this scenario, the trail begins with Cain and evolves into an Absalom spirit the second the jealousy and competition expresses itself in any public manner, even to just one person, usually in the form of offense or victimization. As soon as someone else becomes subject to this, it's the spirit of Absalom that is at work, but the twisted process of getting to this point is the work of the spirit of Cain.

THE SPIRIT OF CAIN

I have been amazed observing how this will begin expressing itself emotionally by sharing a tragic story of injustice, victimization, and wrongdoing. The devil also does not despise the day of small beginnings; he is looking to sow tiny seeds of evil into men and women's hearts that will grow and make way for eventual destruction and death. But the reasoning will always appeal to the intellect, just like it was with Eve in the Garden of Eden. Many times, like Jesus when being tempted, the reasoning will seem spiritual in nature.

I have witnessed this more than once in my lifetime, that a tragedy like this would happen in a place called a sanctuary. However, the enemy never plays nice and is always looking to kill what God has birthed. And that is why we must be so vigilant in this area. The spirit of Cain is a very real spirit of which our hearts must be aware. It seeks to distort our lives, friendships, teams, churches, and ministry relationships.

The Word of God warns us that in the last days brother will turn against brother and people group against people group (Matthew 10:21; Mark 13:8). Be aware of the state of your heart. Always walk with God like David, crying out to Him to examine your heart and reveal to you if there is any wicked root so you can be set free. Pastors, pay attention to these areas in your church and in your leadership team. We are not called to go on a witch-hunt here, but we are encouraged to take heed to examine the state of our flock.

We must all remain humble and realize that Jesus is and always will be the head of the church. If we walk in humility and as servants of the King, then we will avoid destruction. Dissatisfaction, resentment, rivalry, jealousy, and offense are childish and are actually defining where the individual is actually at when it comes to his or her maturity. Oftentimes, these seeds of heart conditions are a test to see if we qualify to be promoted. After all, promotion does not come from the east or from the west, neither does it come from forcing circumstances and warring against our peers or elders—it comes only from the Lord.

Chapter 7

ENVY KILLS THE SON

As we read the Bible and reflect on the story of the birth of Jesus, we become more aware of how this spirit can be at work. Most of us know the beautiful story of how Jesus was born in Bethlehem, how the Son of God descended into the earth and took on the most innocent and vulnerable form of a baby born in an animal barn, lying in a manger. The shepherds were first on the scene, but the wise men would soon follow, though we are not aware of exactly when they arrived to see the young baby Jesus. Some scholars suggest that it was not long after Jesus' birth, while others say that it was almost two years later.

The Magi were more than mere wise men, however—they

were kings from the east who traveled because they followed a star, a sign in the sky. As they drew into the land of Israel, they stopped to meet with Herod, who was the local ruler appointed by the Roman occupation to govern a set territory. They came to Herod innocently thinking that he would share in their wonder for the promised birth of the king the star spoke of and guided them to.

Herod appeared to have great interest in the baby and earnestly asked the wise men to return on the way back and tell him where this baby was so that he could go and worship Him also. But here we begin to see the sadistic tip of the iceberg of the spirit of Cain that was resident in Herod. Imagine for a second an established king who felt threatened by a newborn baby. In Herod's mind, even a rumor or a myth of someone coming to see another promised king or ruler was a huge threat to his identity. History tells us that Herod was actually an Arab who was appointed by the Romans to rule over the Jews. It was a common practice in Roman conquest to put a foreigner, especially a foreigner from a people who hated the conquered land, into a ruling position because that man would rule harshly over the people. And Herod did in fact rule harshly.

Jerusalem was deeply troubled during this time, probably because the sound of a king being born meant a war could break out at any moment and decimate everyone. Another king would challenge the current established authority. They were conquered and were a people of broken spirits with little hopes as far as a nation went. They had troops patrolling their streets every day in battle array. History tells us that the streets were lined with crucified corpses along each side of the road, much like lampposts.

ENVY KILLS THE SON

Anyone who defied or rebelled against the Roman Empire was executed as a warning that any uprising would be met with no mercy. It's here we see Jerusalem troubled at the sound of a possible coming rival king, which could mean a brutal crushing of more of the descendants of Israel. Equally, we see Herod's ego challenged and the spirit of Cain beginning to manifest itself against this rival King.

We read that Herod called the chief priests and scribes to consult to see if this rumor was in fact well founded. And they confirmed the prophecy stating: "But you, Bethlehem, in the land of Judah, are not the least among the rulers of Judah; for out of you shall come a Ruler who will shepherd My people Israel" (Matthew 2:6). Then, without skipping a beat, Herod began to form a game plan by carefully carrying out background research to find out when the star appeared, and then he began to calculate how old this baby would be.

Wanting to know more, Herod summoned the wise men. The wise men were secretly brought before Herod, and he inquired of them to determine what time the star appeared, and he then asked them to return and inform him of the baby's whereabouts so he could go and worship too. The wise men continued on their journey and found the young Jesus and worshiped Him, presenting gifts and showing Jesus great honor. But instead of returning to Herod, "the wise men being warned of God in a dream that they should not return to Herod, they departed into their own country another way" (Matthew 2:12, KJV).

Herod's pride was pricked even further once he learned that the wise men had evaded him and left the country without returning to him with the location of the baby. Herod then proceeded to send out his soldiers to massacre all the male children under two years old, which was according to the age he had calculated from what the wise men had told him. Jealously and competition are willing to murder and eliminate any threat or rival. But it would not be the last time the Son of God saw this in His life. God was miles ahead of Herod's thoughts, and so He divinely warned Joseph in a dream to leave town and escape to Egypt.

Hidden in the details of this beautiful entrance of God becoming Man in order to save the world, we see the opposite of the spirit of Cain at work. We see kings—wise men—who were willing to travel a great distance to come and honor a baby who was to be king. Little did they know that they honored the Son of God in the highest form they knew how while He was in the flesh, in a similar way that Mary would later break open the alabaster box and anoint Jesus' feet. They were also kings of a different sort, but they showed no competition, jealousy, or envy to the newborn King. All we see is honor from these men.

Herod is remembered in infamy as one who without a second thought carried out genocide against a generation of babies who were two years old and younger, all based on envy and competition. Here we see, just like Saul, that the spirit of Cain is not limited to the young and ambitious, but also to the well established and powerful.

This same spirit is furthermore seen throughout the life of Jesus in how He was treated by the Pharisees. Pharisees were the priests of the day who also represented a strong cultural, spiritual, social, and political legalistic standard that was ritualistic in nature and less relational toward Jehovah God. They had held

ENVY KILLS THE SON

these rituals for generations—centuries, in fact. And so when Jesus appeared on the scene, they did not recognize Him as the One fulfilling all the prophecies in the Old Testament Scriptures. The Pharisees were so caught up only seeing that He, in their opinion, defied their culture and claimed to be God's Son that they missed the very Son of God, the fulfillment of Old Testament prophecies, right in their midst.

From the very beginning, the Pharisees knew there was something different about Jesus. They marveled at His words and the answers He gave. But the Pharisees were quite obviously a narcissistic bunch of people. Jesus told them plainly that they loved their high seats and their priestly robes, loving to be called by the titles they had given to themselves as teachers. This statement clearly outlines the platform they had built for themselves, and not only their platform but the way they had begun to enjoy the position and the titles. They loved their titles so much that when God was right in front of them, they did not recognize who it really was that was speaking to them.

These men had a role to represent God to the people and also represent the people to God during the sacrifices and rituals and reading of the Torah. However, they became so intoxicated in their own idea of power and authority that they became jealous of Jesus arriving in town and actually capturing the people's attention with not just His statements but also His deeds that demonstrated great power.

The Pharisees became angry with Jesus, accusing Him of blasphemy—even witchcraft! They accused Him of using the power of the devil in the miraculous deeds He was performing. Why would the representatives of God do this to the Son of God?

THE SPIRIT OF CAIN

It was because their entire identity and social standing was being threatened by a whole new concept of God that Jesus was demonstrating and introducing.

The people of Israel cheered for Jesus more and more, and, like Saul toward David a thousand years before, these priests were infuriated that some man who, to their knowledge, was not a priest was becoming established as a spiritual leader in the community. And it was happening extremely quickly. This was no small house group or private meeting. Rather, Jesus' fame spread throughout the land as He was having crowds of over ten thousand people showing up to His unadvertised spontaneous crusade meetings before Internet, radio, and TV marketing were even possible.

These Pharisees, because of their rigid stance and legalistic beliefs, did not seek out if Jesus truly was the Son of God as He claimed to be; rather, they focused on their jealousy and envy for this Man who, in a short period, had become the talk of the town. Their excuse was that He was blaspheming God. But we know their actual heart motive was that they were jealous and envious of Him. When Pilate asked the crowd if they wanted him to release the King of the Jews, Mark adds in, "For he knew that the chief priests had handed Him over because of envy" (Mark 15:10).

Jesus was performing miracles they had never seen before, casting out devils and talking with authority. But as soon as Jesus claimed to be the Son of God, thus making Himself equal with God, they sought how they could kill Him. Because these men were so religious, they could not see God standing right in front of them in the person of Jesus Christ. They were accustomed to

ENVY KILLS THE SON

being semifeared and revered by the people of Israel, but now they were in second place as Jesus captivated the masses' attention.

Jesus had an amazing moment down at the River Jordan as His cousin John baptized Him and the Father spoke from heaven declaring the identity of Jesus and His pleasure and acceptance of Him right at the beginning of His ministry. To me, this is a picture of Abel's sacrifice being accepted by the Lord. Once there is the acceptance and favor of God on someone's life, it will eventually be evident to all. When people surround and interact with that particular individual, they come across this God-given favor and acceptance and it provokes a response from a heart that is given to jealousy, competition, and envy.

Just as there was a first and second Adam, the second Adam being Christ, so I also see Jesus as the second Abel. He did right before the Father and was accepted; the priests, who had the Torah (or the five books of the law given to Moses by God), had every opportunity to access this great lesson in the story of Cain and Abel. But just like Cain, they became angry and their countenances were fallen. They were commanded to master the sin crouching at their door; they could have chosen to do right before the Lord and be accepted.

But the same spirit that slew Abel entered into the priests as they sought how to slay the Son of God. Jesus knew the spirit that pursued Him; and, unlike Abel who never saw his murderer coming, Jesus was extremely aware of what was going to take place and why it needed to take place. He was also aware of why the Pharisees despised Him to the point of murder.

As the high priest rode home on his donkey from that day when Jesus cried out that it was finished, he, much like

THE SPIRIT OF CAIN

Joseph's brothers after they had rid themselves of their brother and returned to Jacob their father, and also Cain as he was approached by God inquiring where Abel was, claimed complete innocence and absence of knowledge of what had been done. The same spirit that ate fruit from the Tree of the Knowledge of Good and Evil to compete with God, killed Cain, sold Joseph, hunted David, and killed all the baby boys in Bethlehem who were under the age of two, had now crucified the most innocent and favored Man who had ever walked this earth, the Son of God. And all of this happened because of envy and competition; it was all done in the name of justice.

The spirit of Cain desires to be the center of attention. If it cannot have everyone's focus on itself, then it will begin to plot against the person who is the center of attention. And in this case, looking at the life of Jesus, we see mere men, the priests, who were given robes and honor to represent the throne of God, competing against the person of Jesus Christ. Priests, rising out of insecurity because God was getting too much attention and making too many claims that He was God, get to such a progression in their hearts that they killed the Lamb of God, Jesus Christ. The spirit of Cain will stop at nothing until it gets what it desires.

One of my spiritual mothers once told me a story about how she and her husband were moved by God to go on staff in a large church in the South of the United States. Her husband was given a pastoral role and she was hired to work in the church office. She had a strong call to intersession as well, and she was diligent in that call. Her husband was introduced to the pastoral team, and he was also was introduced to the woman who led the intercession ministry. When he met her, it came up in conversation that his wife was also called to intercession.

Immediately, he knew something was wrong, because this woman's face said it all—her countenance fell and she became uneasy. It was so strange, he later said. From that moment on, the woman who was charge of intercession set out to intimidate and inhibit my spiritual mom from feeling included. She became so insecure at the thought of having another mature intercessor in the group; it became apparent she was an obvious threat to this woman. It came to the point that she started making statements like, "I'm in charge of this group and don't think you can come and take over," when my spiritual mom was innocently there with the sole intention to link arms and join in prayer for God to move.

This woman became more and more hostile toward my spiritual mom, making her feel less and less welcome, which was all due to the fact that she valued being "in charge" rather than part of a team of people who loved God and were there to serve Him. Years later, this woman left the church and statements she made revealed to everyone what was really in her heart toward other people around her.

Leaders must always remember that leading people is an act of serving and lifting others up, not standing in a position and using "followers" for validation. Even the disciples were at times in rivalry against each other for position and favor. One day, the mother of two of the disciples tried asking Jesus to seat her sons on either side of His throne. Competition and ambition are nasty things internally in the human mind, but when it goes a step further and is actually vocalized, it provokes others with similar tendencies to increase their engagement into competition. This becomes a debased mindset in which the individual has a mentality of a dog-eat-dog independent survival. It's a kill-or-be-killed perception, but not a reality.

The primal instinct of survival is appealed to, which engages a poverty mind-set that Cain operated in, that dictates that there's not enough favor to go around, so I better do everything in my power to obtain the only bit of favor there is. The disciples in the early days must have been like little children squabbling over who would be the best at times, have the most, or who had impressed Jesus as the greatest. It is so easy to see this in other people, but human nature is consistent—we do the same things ourselves, oftentimes without even recognizing it.

The Jewish culture was well accustomed to discipleship during the time of Jesus (i.e., the school of the prophets, for instance, in the days of Elijah and Elisha). These disciples of Jesus knew someone great was schooling them, but it was only later in the relationship that they began to realize that He was the Son of God. There would have been many occasions where they would have seen their relationship with Jesus similar to the renowned school of the prophets, and in many ways they assumed the role of students. They did call Jesus teacher and master more than anything else. In this environment competition was evident.

Can you imagine Judas reveling in the moment that Jesus rebuked Peter, saying, "Get behind me, Satan"? In that moment, his competition would have dictated that he was now a step higher than the brash disciple. And yet Jesus rebuked Judas himself in a far gentler manner when Judas protested about the alabaster box being broken and poured over Jesus, claiming

ENVY KILLS THE SON

that the money should have been given to the poor instead. The beginning of offense and entitlement in Judas's heart can be seen here, in which the seed of rivalry began, with Judas thinking he knew more than everyone else. I don't believe Judas sold Jesus for money, otherwise he would have never given the money back.

Consider this: Judas was born of the same tribe as Jesus, the promised lineage that the Messiah would come from—the line of Judah. We also know that Judas was a thief, but isn't it interesting that the Bible tells us that the devil entered Judas before he betrayed Jesus? I'm sure sin was crouching at the door of his heart. And although he did not murder Jesus directly, his betrayal definitely empowered it. I wonder to what extent Judas had envy and jealousy toward the Son of God, making his betrayal that much more rational in the heart of the man Jesus described as the son of perdition, or son of hell?

When the seventy came back with joy, marveling at the miracles they had just performed, Jesus immediately addressed and rearranged their thinking so as not to rejoice in the miracles themselves but rather to rejoice in the fact that their names were written in heaven. This is a great perspective into the fallen heart of humanity and how far off we can be from heaven's ideals and priorities. If you really want to see what is in a person, give him or her power. Jesus' disciples were rejoicing about miracles and signs and wonders, demons obeying their very word, which is both amazing and dangerous. It is amazing in that they were able to partner in heaven's authority, and it was dangerous because egos and identities were starting to become distorted.

In these moments in which individuals operate in the power of God, it is easy to forget who supplies the power. The power being demonstrated does not validate the one facilitating it. Rather, the power validates the awesomeness and greatness of God. But in these moments, it is so easy to lose focus and take credit and begin to compare your gift with another's to somehow place a value on how great an individual is; or, in another light, to see another operating in the power of God who may be a peer, and you have watched them grow into their gifts and anointing, possibly even excelling your gifts and anointing.

What we fail to understand so many times is that the offices and gifts are for the edification of the church body. If someone has a gift, it is there to serve the body, not elevate a particular individual above another. You will hear many great men and women of God talk about people wanting their mantles or anointing, but they don't understand what it has cost them to get there. Many people become jealous and threatened at someone else growing or excelling in their gifts and anointing, especially someone they are familiar with.

When Jesus began His ministry, not everyone rejoiced with Him. Some were saying, "Is this not the kid from up the street, Mary and Joseph's son?" It's that kind of familiarity that refuses to see someone excelling in an area because it's a threat to the person. And how could someone who grew up down the street be better than me? This is a prime example of the mind-set found in many Christians today.

The objective for many people is to be at the top, and this is purely earthly, sensual, and demonic in nature, having only the appearance of wisdom. In heaven's culture, and in God's perfect plan for the body of Christ, everyone is content and honored to be in his or her delegated position or role. Not everyone can be the foot, or the bride would just be one giant foot; in the same way, not everyone can be the head or there would just be one giant head, which is again a bizarre distortion of reality.

Jesus is the only head of the church, both the local church and the worldwide church, and no one can take His place. We all need to have something in us that presses forward into our upward call in glory with our eyes focused only on Jesus, not measuring ourselves by our leaders or our peers. There are positions and authority in the body of Christ, and this is not in any way taking away from that; however, positions and authority do not affect levels of worth.

A true leader and mature son or daughter will understand that as they progress in their walk with God they are being transformed into more of a servant. Great leaders are great servers. They do not find their identity or worth in their followers; rather, they speak affirmation, empowerment, and worth into the ones they lead. This is why the Bible says to give double honor to those who labor in the Word and serve us, which is not encouraging any form of devaluing or familiarity. It also tells us that the greatest in the kingdom will be servants of all. Jesus is the greatest servant who ever walked the earth, so He is worthy of all our honor. Great servants do not compete—they serve.

We cannot have envy and jealousy while operating in a pure form of serving. Humility is the key, for it corrects wrong perspectives of pride and competition. We must allow the Spirit of God to search us out on a regular basis if we are to be free from this competition. If we are really going to be imitators of Jesus, then we must love the truth, and sometimes truth will challenge our very motives and corner our actual intentions.

THE SPIRIT OF CAIN

David cried out to God and prayed, "Search me, O God, and know my heart; try me, and know my anxieties; and see if there is any wicked way in me, and lead me in the way everlasting" (Psalm 139:23–24). I would encourage you to ask the same of God, for Him to search you and see if there is anything within you that is prone to competition or jealousy. It matters to God why we do what we do, think what we think, and say what we say.

When we look at the double-edged sword of God that divides soul and spirit, bone and marrow, as well as the thoughts and intentions of our heart, then we begin to see that God really does pay attention to our motives and intentions. Ask yourself, why do I want to do this, or why do I have an aspiration to do this or that, or why do I want to be the best at that? Or why do I want to hold the microphone in church; why do I want to be in that position of power? The answer may surprise you as you invite God to search your heart.

Chapter 8

OVERCOMING THE SPIRIT OF CAIN

The experience of personally having to walk through a few situations in which the spirit of Cain was operating in another person has given me a great deal of perspective and wisdom from the Lord on how to respond when confronted with this demonic spirit. First, in case this has never happened to you, I will describe the experience in a way that is easy to imagine.

The spirit of Cain is a predatory spirit in its outworking. You will never understand how a person, who has set himself or herself against you, came to the conclusion to do so, nor all that has all happened in their mind to bring them to this point. They have simply not taken every thought captive that has come into their mind, and this evil spirit has seeded them with jealousy, envy,

THE SPIRIT OF CAIN

and competition. You will never understand how they arrived at the destination to have such aggression toward you. But you do need to understand that they went through quite a process to get there, a process of overriding the law of love and the voice of the Holy Spirit.

I can say that most often when I have seen this spirit at work, the person already had the seeds of it in his or her life, formed into their emotional DNA years prior. But in each case, there was a slow transition from mild and undetected envy into a blatant competitive contention that in some cases displayed extreme character assassination. In all these cases, however, these were people I was close to and loved dearly. They were people I trusted.

Have you ever been in a situation in which there are three people and one reward, and you happened to be the person who received the reward? It really blessed you, but one or both of the other two people had a glaring jealousy toward you that caused you to feel bad that you were the one who received the reward. It probably made you feel resented; or maybe you felt an overwhelming pressure because of the other's extreme desire for the reward to the point of feeling levels of hostility from them. The other two were your friends, but during this time you started to realize they were not really that friendly and purely living for themselves.

The spirit of Cain expresses itself like one country going to war with another purely because it has a resource that the invading country does not have. It behaves like sharks circling a swimmer, waiting for just the right moment to attack. The spirit of Cain behaves like a wolf lurking in the shadows just waiting for a victim to take a nap, or someone wanting to hurt you for

OVERCOMING THE SPIRIT OF CAIN

no apparent reason at all. The spirit of Cain feels like someone waiting for you to make a mistake so it can expose your failure and disqualify you, while at the same time presenting themselves as the only suitable replacement.

It is like the kid who grew up being teased at school, forever after holding vengeance in his or her heart to show the world that he or she would be better than everyone else. And that unhealed heart picked wars in his or her mind with anyone who represented a person of success, someone who was better than him or her, anyone who made him or her feel inferior, or any obstacle to his or her goals. A lot of unsuspecting people suffered as a result. The spirit of Cain is like the one kid in class who had to be the center of attention, no matter what had to be done to retain that attention. It is nothing more than a dishonoring spirit.

I have experienced all of these feelings emanating from people operating in the spirit of Cain. It's a difficult thing at times because you cannot necessarily pin it down to one expression or manifestation—it's a subtle and not so obvious politically positioned interaction that takes place. Have you ever heard the expression "the wolf is at the door"? The spirit of Cain is like that in the same way that God warned Cain: "Sin crouches at your door, but you must rule over it " (Genesis 4:7). God was describing the spirit of Cain as we now see it manifested today in our day and time. It crouches and lies in wait for the opportune time, and then it pounces at a moment of vulnerability to take advantage of or to damage another.

For reasons rooted in competition, the spirit of Cain has accumulated a list of reasons to hate. It is looking to express that pent-up vengeance all in spite of another's reward for doing what is right. It's like the kid who failed his exam and hated the kid who studied really hard and passed. The spirit has an air that will first express itself toward you in a competitive way that is more than just friendly competition, then it will cause you to experience an air of threat and passive-aggressive tension. Be careful of people who associate their identity with competition.

Although this spirit isn't always overtly obvious in its jealousy and competition, it can be in some cases. There will come a point in which you will begin to experience a feeling of pressure coming from another person, and this is not to get something from you—it's because of who you are perceived to be in their mind. This will likely be in the form of a threat against their security or ability to climb the ladder, whatever that ladder is. In some cases it can even begin with flattery. As time goes on, however, it evolves and may become more cunning and sophisticated. You cannot allow the agenda of this spirit to draw you into its web, which is right where it wants you.

Something I have learned the hard way in my walk with God is this: we are made up of the old man, which is our flesh, and the renewed man, which is our spirit. When we walk and respond from our renewed spirit that is communing with God on a regular basis, the devil cannot touch us. But the devil is not trying to communicate to our renewed spirit man. The devil is constantly trying to communicate and provoke our old man, our flesh. He will press on ego or pride or the rights we think we have; he will work on offending us and causing us to feel threatened by this spirit operating through someone else.

This spirit's entire goal is to distract our attention away from walking in and responding to the Spirit with God. It longs to

OVERCOMING THE SPIRIT OF CAIN

draw us out from the covering of the protective shadow of the Almighty, causing us to momentarily forget that we are sons and daughters of God, thus provoking us to respond out of our carnal or fleshly man. When we do this, we have been set up in a trap.

In the Introduction of this book, I mentioned a young man who confronted me and told me that God was going to give him my jacket. Well, as the years progressed, we both grew in God, both had struggles and weaknesses to overcome, and also amazing victories in Jesus. But throughout the years I never forgot God's warning about our relationship being comparable to that of Cain and Abel. There were countless times in which this man assassinated my character behind the scenes to our pastor, all with the motive of being favored and promoted. And each time I had to choose to respond in the flesh or in the Spirit.

You see, young men and women are full of zeal and passion to grow and excel in God—but selfish ambition mixed into that creates a nasty cocktail of heart conditions that will cause good people to do bad things. This young man was fixated on being a famous minister. In fact, he would constantly watch video clips of all the well-known ministers preaching and teaching, which in itself is a good thing. But several times he told me he was studying these men so he could be the best. It was well beyond being merely unhealthy—it was a vain obsession of his. He saw everyone as someone to be beat. He had trained his heart to see through these filters.

I grew in my relationship with the Lord within my local church, knowing God had personally called me. But I was in an environment in which it felt like I had a hungry dog "snapping at my ankles." There were countless occasions in which this young man was itching to prove himself more worthy and superior to me in his call. My pastor would come and have big talks with me due to things this other person had told him that were skewed and twisted all with the purpose of getting ahead of me and being seen as the favored son. He even used the opportunity and spoke from the pulpit one service about how he had to "keep his heart right because I was so offensive to him," as I sat on the front row. Needless to say, it was a painful experience for me.

I had never tried to hurt this young man at all. I had no bad feelings toward him. But I was beginning to see more clearly that he had such intense competition toward me that everything I said and did was being studied, to see if he could find any flaws and weaknesses. He was looking for excuses to become easily offended at me because his heart was already set against me. As this behavior continued, it affected my perception of our relationship and I found myself being less vulnerable to him and pulling away from a close relationship with him, knowing that his motive was to push me down in order for him to step up.

I talked to the Lord about this a great deal during this time as, you could probably imagine, it was a huge bother to me. As I mentioned earlier in the book, I never went to complain to my pastor because that would have caused more problems, so I left it with God and waited for Him to move on my behalf. God assured me several times not to respond to this man's behavior because competition has a pull that demands a competitive response. If competition meets competition, then you have a small war on your hands.

If you are experiencing the effects of the spirit of Cain in your own life, then you do not need to react and engage in competition. True sons and daughters of heaven don't need to defend their identity; they simply stand in who they are in God. You don't need to defend yourself—just walk humbly and go about your life and walk with God. God is a God of justice, and He will ensure that you are vindicated. But it is important to let Him do it in His time—not your timing. Sometimes, as unpleasant as things may be, God allows adversity to fashion us into better people. Whenever we respond in the flesh, we lose authority. We give up the spiritual high ground and authority the moment we respond with an eye-for-eye mentality.

A major trait of this spirit is that it will try and strike you in a vulnerable area and eliminate you from being competition in the particular individual's mind. Seeing this in another person will engage your basic self-defense mechanisms. Therefore, if this happens, you must remember that you actually do not have the right to strike back. Jesus is your vindicator; Jesus is your defender and the One who will obtain justice for you. He said that vengeance belongs to Him. If you ever begin to embark on setting the record straight or getting vengeance on a Cain spirit, God will not be able to vindicate you, for your actions will have robbed Him of that right.

To some degree, this is a crucifixion experience in which you will need to allow the accusers to afflict you. I am by no means suggesting we tolerate abuse here. But during the times when a Cain spirit has really gone out of its way to assassinate my credibility or my position, even though it would be easy to retaliate I have remained silent. I allowed God's justice to play out in His timing, not mine. I have definitely not always

THE SPIRIT OF CAIN

responded perfectly, for, just like you, I also am a work in progress. If you haven't responded correctly in the past, it is important to learn from your mistakes and move on, while not feeling condemned.

In the time of Jesus, it was the spirit of Cain that drove the Pharisees' hatred of Jesus. They were jealous of the fact that Jesus was not part of what they considered the priesthood in the temple, and yet, in three short years, Jesus gained more fame and notoriety than these priests. The people of Israel flocked to Him, and signs and wonders that only God could work followed everywhere He went. The Pharisees sacrificed like Cain in their religious tradition, but when they saw Jesus respected by God like Abel was while they remained not respected, it only fueled their hatred. This led to character assassination and a plot to kill the Son of God, just like Cain assassinated Abel in his heart until he felt justified to physically kill him.

As Jesus stood before His accusers, He was silent—He chose not to respond to them and vindicate Himself. And herein lies a key for all of us who encounter the spirit of Cain: sometimes God will allow someone to attack us, but God is not looking for us to retaliate with weapons of the same kind. The greatest thing we can do is stay humble, not engaging and becoming aggressive in our response or trying to fight or confront this in our own power or strength. Most importantly, we cannot respond in any spirit of competition. Rather, we must continually bring this person before the Lord and pray for his or her healing. At the same time, we need to enter into spiritual warfare against the spirit operating in and through that person, using the authority of the blood of Jesus to strip the spirit of Cain of its power, which is the "blood of

OVERCOMING THE SPIRIT OF CAIN

sprinkling that speaks better things than that of Abel" (Hebrews 12:24).

The blood of Jesus is the most powerful key of freedom against this spirit. The blood Jesus shed for the sins of humanity answered the blood of Abel. Instead of vengeance against the spirit of Cain, we now have the ability to respond like Jesus did, with forgiveness and humility, to people operating in the spirit of Cain. Understanding that a deep emotional wound has probably accompanied that person since childhood, tormenting them and driving them—they are actually in desperate need of freedom and do not even realize it.

Whenever we encounter a spirit of Cain, we are either perceived as a competitor for something yet to be attained or have been given, or we have come into something that they do not have, and so they have spite toward us as a result. We need to ask God the Father for wisdom in this area in order to navigate around this spirit and to remain untouched. It is important to understand that God has allowed all of this so you may be tested and refined, all for the purpose of bringing out gold that has been through the fire, so we are mature and stable in the Spirit of God. It's an open book test, and God will help us with all the answers and assist us if we simply choose to walk in the Spirit.

Time and experience have taught me to be quick to forgive when it comes to encountering this spirit. Do not rehearse over and over again the offense of this person's agreement with the spirit of Cain or you may be drawn into operating in the same spirit. Many times, for my own personal well-being, I have needed to withdraw levels of relationship from these people for a season so I could protect my own heart. This is not a response

THE SPIRIT OF CAIN

that is founded in rejection, but rather one that is based on the Scripture: "Make no friendship with an angry man, and with a furious man do not go" (Proverbs 22:24).

An individual's behavior determines the level of intimacy in any form of relationship. Many times, but not at all times, these people have remained in my life but there has been a distancing in relationship. Over time things improve as I have slowly reconnected and trust was rebuilt. But if something was done so psychotic in the operation of this evil spirit, and I have known a couple of people in which this has been the case, then I have felt led by the Spirit of God to withdraw altogether from that person.

Please know that I am not suggesting we cut people out of our lives purely because they are caught up in a wrong spirit for a time. The Spirit of God must lead us in each and every case. In every person we encounter who has this spirit, the law of love must be our response. Sometimes we need to also apply the law of love to ourselves too, not just to the person who is under the influence of this spirit. And sometimes distance is needed in order to protect ourselves and families from destructive people.

One of the agendas of the spirit of Cain will be to operate in competition and jealousy toward you with the intent of provoking you to respond in the same manner, causing you to shift into jealousy and competition. When responded to in this way, it does nothing but create wars and division in your life and obstructs you from the true blessing of God. Or its intent is to simply remove or take from you what God has freely given to you.

As you have read, I have had to deal with several lengthy instances of the spirit of Cain coming against me over the years. It's a horrible experience when you feel pressed by the unspoken jealousy, ambition, and competition of another person. Having an uneasy knowing that you are resented for who you are or what you have, and that because of this perception you have become the benchmark to beat, is hard to take. It happens in the workplace, sporting world, in any number of relational aspects of life, and also the church. And the spiritual environment in which this takes place is by far the most sinister.

Some of the greatest atrocities in the history of the world have taken place due to a misconception of God's true nature. You see, God has no limits to His person or His generosity—He is not a human being. God's love is described in the Bible in such a way that you cannot define its volume; you cannot quantify how endless and limitless His love is. How is it that brother will fight against brother because of a perception that there is only one winner, or only enough love for one person to receive? The amazing counterculture with God's nature in contrast to the world is that God's love can cause every person to become a winner and favored son or daughter. One doesn't have to lose if another is to win.

The spirit of Cain robs a person of God's peace to rest in their own identity, and so they then look at the Abel in their life who is doing well, who has the favor of God, and against that person they set out to vent their rejection and strike out in frustration. This is in order to get something that would be theirs anyway if they just did what was right before the Lord.

I have been astounded at the lengths certain people have gone to throughout my journey to compete against the favor that God has placed on my life. The aggression with which an individual operates against you is driven by insecurity and a lack of peace,

THE SPIRIT OF CAIN

and it attempts to provoke you to respond in the same degenerated spirit. Naturally, part of your human survival instinct wants to defend who you are or what you have as a response to the resulting feeling of threat that comes from others operating in this spirit.

God has taught me over the years that the best response is no response at all. Sometimes He allows pressure and even persecution to crucify our old nature, and in the process refine us to reflect more and more of His character. If you determine to put Jesus first, continue on the path and assignment God has set you on, and don't respond to the person operating in the competitive spirit of Cain, it will lose its power over your life.

I have also seen in some cases, despite the pain that it can cause you, going out of your way to love the person competing against you. This can defuse the situation and transform an enemy into a friend. Never underestimate the power of God. However, love is not stupid! In some cases you need to flee from a person who is not healthy for you. But always go the way of humility and take the low road, for then you will remain safe. And always remember that justice, vengeance, and vindication are God's job, not yours.

Don't ever allow envy and competition from others to cause you to back away from soaring in your gifts and excelling in your call. The way others choose to behave toward you cannot be allowed to dictate your confidence in the blessings of God that He has given to you. Walk confidently in everything God is doing in your life, enjoy it, and abound in what you have been given. And always remember to stay humble and don't back down.

Being resentful of another person because they have what

you do not is not good for your soul. When what another has dictates your personal self-worth, it is an extremely unhealthy state to be in. This trait of jealousy and competition is something that has plagued fallen humanity since the time of Adam and Eve. Just as God said to Cain, "Sin is crouching at your door. It's desire is for you, but you must rule over it and master it," so God is saying to us today when talking about the spirit of Cain.

Every day we are presented with opportunities to become resentful because of what others have, which can be either materially or positionally. And every day we have the choice to become angry and wear a fallen countenance when others receive honor and favor, which is especially true if it is something we have really desired for our own lives. But feeding this demonic voice will only, and always only, end in destruction and shame.

God asked Cain, "If you do well, will you not be accepted?" (Genesis 3:7). And herein lies another key to getting free from this spirit that so permeates our lives and the culture of the church. Each of us must take our eyes off of another's progress, successes, and accolades. If we are constantly focusing on what another has, then we have been allowing their blessings and rewards for doing right in God's sight communicate an element of failure into our own inner identities. But if we compare ourselves with ourselves, then we become unwise.

The spirit of Cain is actually a trap to people who have attempted to be successful or obtain God's blessing and have got it wrong. God wants you to try again and get it right so you can be accepted in the thing that you desire to grow in. But the spirit of Cain is the decoy to take your eyes off of God in these moments, and instead to take out your frustration on your neighbor who

THE SPIRIT OF CAIN

is doing well before the Lord, or who has been blessed with the favor of people and who is experiencing promotion. This spirit will fanatically attempt to pull you away from doing what is right before God, causing you to take up arms against your brother or sister instead. It is important to see this and sidestep the trap.

I love to go fishing, especially after game fish, like tuna. Now if the bait or the lure were not so attractive to the fish, then I would probably not catch any fish at all. But I can assure you that I get the best bait I can buy in order to lure the fish onto my hook and fill my icebox with fresh fish. The enemy has the same mentality when it comes to getting people to bite his bait. We need to see this spirit for what it is, and we need to ask the Holy Spirit to set us free from any habitual biases we have toward this mentality of unhealthy competition and rivalry.

You must ask God to create a clean heart and renew a right spirit within you, just as David did when he sinned against the Lord (Psalm 51:10). It may also be helpful to ask your pastor or a trusted friend for deliverance and counsel as well. Humble yourself before the Lord and ask someone who is safe, mature, and well grounded in your church or fellowship to tell you if they see these tendencies in you. A lot of the time our hearts deceive us, but the Bible tells us our friend will be able to search us out (Proverbs 18:17).

Take back for yourself the innocence of simply being God's son or the Father's daughter. Stop looking to others out of insecurity to somehow gauge where you are at in the pecking order, or the hierarchical order, for this is both carnal and demonic. The Word of God instructs us to prefer others above ourselves: "Let nothing be done through selfish ambition or conceit, but in lowliness of mind let each esteem others better than himself" (Philippians 2:3). Don't you think God seeing you honor others before yourself and genuinely celebrating others' successes will get His attention and motivate Him to want to bless you all the more?

We must look to Jesus, who is the author and finisher of our faith (Hebrews 12:1–2). He is the scriptwriter and director of our personal story, if we allow Him to direct our steps. If we struggle with jealousy and competition, then we may need to discipline ourselves not to get so caught up in reading other people's stories that we do not became dissatisfied with our own journey and resentful of theirs.

The agenda of the spirit of Cain is to cause us to devalue and disdain God's instruction to us, to have us walk in the flesh, and to despise our brothers or sisters in Christ, eventually having an outworking in which we come against our brother or sister. If we can keep our eyes fixed on Jesus, then all the other distractions will lose their power and we can then focus our energy into doing what is right and being accepted by God. It is our desire that God is released and empowered to accept and respect us, like He did Abel.

It's amazing how "there is a way that seems right to a man, but its end is the way of death" (Proverbs 14:12). We must leave our feelings and follow the way that God set out so clearly for Cain to do right and be accepted in His sight. If you have been tormented by this spirit, or even lived in agreement with the spirit of Cain in your own life, then there is good news for you. The name of Jesus is above every other name. There is freedom and healing available for you.

You may need to sit down and list the people you have had aggression against and a heart of unhealthy competition toward. It may only be one person, or it could be many individuals. Once you write down those names, then you need to humble yourself before the Lord and ask Him to reveal your heart. As God begins to reveal circumstances around each person and situation that comes to mind, be honest with yourself and God. Allow yourself to see what has taken place in your heart and repent before the Lord. To *repent* means to change your way of thinking. You may need to repent and apologize to the very people you have resented and competed against. In some cases, you may need to put things right. Once you have repented, then it is important to ask the Lord to deliver you of any demonic oppression from the spirit of Cain. Command it to leave your life in the name of Jesus.

Finally, ask the Lord to help you walk in freedom and have a renewed mind. Romans 12:2 is a good Scripture benchmark key emphasizing the need to continually be refreshed and transformed in your mind and your thinking: "And do not be conformed to this world, but be transformed by the renewing of your mind, that you may prove what is that good and acceptable and perfect will of God."

If you are reading this book, and what is being described outlines the issues of your heart you are currently struggling with, then you must understand that the spirit of Cain is a seed that wants to grow in your heart until you rise up against the person or people God has called you to celebrate and empower. Most people don't find it easy to discipline their emotions in this area, but their emotions must be mastered.

OVERCOMING THE SPIRIT OF CAIN

We need to discipline our emotions because this is where the seed of the spirit of Cain will lodge within our person. Offense is not an intellectual issue, but rather an emotional one. I heard a minister once make this statement some time ago: "I need to be so dead to me that I am dead to you." He was not suggesting that we become heartless beings, but rather that we become so dead to our flesh that when another person does something that has the potential to hurt or offend us, we don't "feel" it anymore.

God calls us to bring every thought captive into the knowledge of Christ; every crazy human emotional thought must be processed through the filter of Jesus. Offense, competition, jealousy, rivalry, and every other fallen concept cannot make it through the filter of Jesus. If we don't have Jesus filtering our minds, then we will be subject to every evil and sinful suggestion that come from demonic spirits. We can be rest assured that it is God's desire that we are free from the influence of this spirit in our lives. We have been given the power and the tools to be free in Jesus' name.

> For though we walk in the flesh, we do not war according to the flesh. For the weapons of our warfare are not carnal but mighty in God for pulling down strongholds, casting down arguments and every high thing that exalts itself against the knowledge of God, bringing every thought into captivity to the obedience of Christ.
> —2 CORINTHIANS 10:3–5

Unhealthy competition, envy, rivalry, and jealousy are the perfect gateway for the spirit of Cain to have access into an

THE SPIRIT OF CAIN

individual's life. This is why God was encouraging Cain to do right after his countenance had fallen and he had become angry with his brother. God's warning was that sin was crouching at his door. This predatory spirit was waiting at Cain's heart for the opportunity when Cain's will and hatred were fully yielded, making him an agreeable party to the demonic influence.

These sins are the entry to this murderous spirit. God's Word tells us, "Above all else, guard your heart, for from it flow the issues of life" (Proverbs 4:23). If you allow darkness into your heart, darkness will express itself through you. You must shield and protect yourself from this type of wickedness by building God's Spirit, Word, and commandments into your heart so you can withstand the enemy.

Chapter 9

INNER IDENTITY AND HUMILITY

One of the oldest questions ever asked is, "Who am I and why am I here?" Humanity lost more than innocence the day Adam and Eve sinned by eating from the Tree of the Knowledge of Good and Evil—we lost the natural inherent knowledge of who we really are at the core of our being. This can be immediately seen in action in the story of Cain and Abel, which is just one generation after Adam and Eve were kicked out of the Garden of Eden.

To truly know who we are, we need to know who God is. If we don't have a right understanding about God, about His nature and His attributes, then we cannot understand who we are as beings created in His image. A child who grows up in a warm and nurturing family, intimately knowing their parents love them not by knowledge but rather by sight, hearing, and touch, that same child truly knows who they are. His or her parents' love brings a security to that little child's heart of who Mom and Dad are, then, almost automatically, a security and level of identity is present in that child.

The drastic contrast to this is a child who never knew his or her parents, a child who has never met them before. Maybe this child was raised in an orphanage and then fostered in their early years but never experienced genuine love. This child will naturally be left wondering where they came from and who they are because they didn't grow up in a stable family. I know a few people who have had this as their story and were radically healed and authentic identity was evident in their lives because of their intimacy with the Father.

No matter what type of family we grow up in, however, the truth is that our circumstances in childhood or throughout life, whether good or bad, can never ultimately define who we are. They are mere environmental ingredients that contribute toward our shaping as individuals who have been created in the image of God.

Let us now consider the difference between a person who is intimate with Father God and one who is not. The difference between these two individuals is like the difference between night and day. Those who are intimate with God are increasingly secure in who they are. In seeing who God is, there is also a place in which we realize why we exist. Therefore, we look to God to get our identity and not to someone or something else. Circumstances, privileges, positions, and possessions no longer

INNER IDENTITY AND HUMILITY

define who we are as people. Competition no longer is in effect as another's blessing does not change our identity.

Competition, envy, and jealousy can only be engaged in when a true knowing and rest in who we are is not present. I can only be jealous when something you have makes me feel lesser or insufficient. Because I don't feel good about who I am, I feel forced to frantically compete with who you are in order to feel like I am a valid human being. Once we get a revelation of the value Jesus truly delivered on Calvary for our freedom, then we will stop thinking in this way.

In my young adult years, I experienced a great deal of shame and rejection. One day I heard the Holy Spirit speak to me, saying, "The bodyguard of shame and rejection is pride, and pride can wear many faces." God was helping me understand that I had pride operating in my heart as a defense mechanism to the massive shame I had walked through in certain circumstances with my family. When shame and rejection are present, insecurity most definitely will be present as well. And when insecurity is present, pride will automatically be working to compensate for perceived failures or insufficiencies. This will begin a somewhat aggressive contending for an appearance of excelling or success. This aggression doesn't have to be overtly bold in nature—it can also be extremely passive.

I have met some amazingly talented men who were intelligent and handsome, but who were shorter than maybe they wanted to be in height. Although these men have so much going for them, they feel an overwhelmingly strong sense to prove themselves as successful or even superior individuals. They feel this way not because they have focused on their God-given talents and gifts, but rather because they have focused on others instead of who God made them to be. Because of this, they have experienced a level of shame and insecurity; subsequently, pride is present to compensate and prove to the world that they are just as tall as any other man. This pride is usually expressed in the form of chopping someone else down in size, whether that is emotionally, intellectually, or from a character-assassination standpoint.

This is a tragic cycle that stems from someone who doesn't know who they are in Christ. And because they don't know who they are or why they were created, it progresses on to hurt another person. But identity and humility present in a person's life will detour this from happening. Let's be honest with ourselves: we all have things that at times make us feel insecure. But knowing who we really are in Christ makes those things not become our identity givers. They may be annoying at times, but they will certainly not dictate our worth or value when we are occupied with looking into the eyes of a loving Father.

Identity is not what you do or what perceived defects you have; identity is who God says you are. If you don't know who God says you are, then humble yourself, abandon your self-defense, your self-provider mechanisms, and seek Him with your whole heart. As you spend time daily seeking God, then He will tell you who you are and who you were created to be.

Assess your life and look at what or who you are allowing to dictate your worth or identity. Are you getting your worth and identity from what you do, from what you own, or you what you seemingly lack in life? Are you getting your identity by trying to measure up to what your neighbor has? Or are you getting your

INNER IDENTITY AND HUMILITY

worth and identity from God alone, by gazing into the eyes of Jesus? You may need to make some adjustments so that He—and He alone—is defining who you are. God is the only One qualified to do that.

I often tell my church that when great men or women affirm me or honor me, that is a complement, but when God affirms me or speaks worth into my life, that is my identity. And we would all do well to know the difference between the two. Many times people place too great a value on what others say and think about them. There is no actual merit in building an identity or security based on what others say about you. Pride will always precede destruction and heartache. This is why the Bible says, "Pride goes before destruction" (Proverbs 16:18).

Pride is scary in that it blinds the person who has it. When pride is in operation in our lives, it will be noticeable to most other people but us. That is why we need our neighbor to come search us out spiritually and bring accountability into our lives. The disturbing truth in this area is that when competition and jealousy are present, we will not let another come and search out our heart, as it will expose us as vulnerable human beings.

Competition is much like a race. Vulnerability is like letting the opponent have the opportunity to see something that may disqualify us from winning, which is an incredibly dangerous place to be in. As bizarre as it may sound, far more Christians have pride in operation in their hearts and minds than would like to admit. The Bible says in Proverbs, "A man who isolates himself seeks his own desire, he rages against all wise judgment" (Proverbs 18:1). Humility is the beginning of wisdom, because it positions the person for the favor of God and makes a him or

THE SPIRIT OF CAIN

her teachable. God draws near to the humble, but He is repelled from the proud.

How do I humble myself before God so I am no longer in danger of being prideful? Well, the fear of the Lord is a great place to start. The Holy Spirit taught me something early on in my walk with Him: we need to take regular time to recognize just how great and big and awesome God actually is. Then we will see ourselves in perspective—we are like mere ants God fell in love with. If we can regularly see this truth with this frame of mind, then we will begin to see the greatness of God and the smallness of ourselves, being so dependent on Him, which is a great place to begin humility.

Intimacy with God causes humility to be present in our lives that nothing else can create. Obviously, there are so many faces of pride, such as false humility, which is pretending to be humble but actually wanting all the praise and glory; spiritual pride, which is taking pride in our spiritual status; arrogant pride, which is presuming ourselves to be great in our own eyes; and the pride of life, which is pride in our own lives. There is also a pride of strength—in our own strength and ability—which denies God's strength and assumes the role of god in our thoughts and actions. We can be proud of our riches, pride in what we have and own, and we can also be proud in our poverty, which is pride in what we are giving up for God's sake.

No matter what type of pride we have, we need to exchange it for humility or we will be positioned for a hard fall. There is only one face of humility, and that is one bowed before the King of Kings and Lord of Lords. Instead of being proud, we need to

INNER IDENTITY AND HUMILITY

focus our desire for worth on the God who knows our name and knows the number of hairs on our head. We must constantly look to Jesus, the firstborn of all the sons and daughters of God, to find our identity.

One of the Scriptures that I have marveled at many times is John 18:3–6:

> Then Judas, having received a detachment of troops, and officers from the chief priests and Pharisees, came there with lanterns, torches, and weapons. Jesus therefore, knowing all things that would come upon Him, went forward and said to them, "Whom are you seeking?" They answered Him, "Jesus of Nazareth." Jesus said to them, "I am He." And Judas, who betrayed Him, also stood with them. Now when He said to them, "I am He," they drew back and fell to the ground.

Jesus had been travailing in the garden, praying for this cup of suffering to pass from Him. He was intimately conversing with the Father over the weightiest matter and the very purpose of His birth. He had spent a great deal of time with the Father during His life so that everything He did was ordered and planned by His Father. And in the moment that Judas, the traitor, arrived in the garden with the troop of soldiers, we see a demonstration of what heavenly identity produces.

The guard called out, "Are you Jesus?" Jesus stepped forward and simply replied, "I am He." With those words, a surge of God's power flew through that garden and the entire troop of soldiers were all knocked to the ground. The potency of Jesus' intimate knowledge of His actual identity caused heaven to be released into their hearts that night in a way that radically impacted the guards.

The call to find our identity in God alone is a call for every single son and daughter of the Father, a call to be so intimate with the Father that we also receive the potency of our identity from Him alone. This is so that we too can release heaven into our world and surroundings.

The question must be asked, how do we put a stop to the enemy's established culture and mind-set? How do we change the cultural tide and renew our minds in a way that glorifies God? If we look to the ultimate example, Jesus, who made Himself of no reputation, who became a little lower than the angels, and who was born in a muddy barn that featured every sort of animal smell and noise, it is then that we can begin to see the manifestation of a different culture. Jesus did not show up on the earth and cut others down; He was not envious or jealous of anyone; He did not come to compete with anyone.

Jesus was the perfect picture of what it looks like to walk in one's identity and security in the Father. He was the manifest example in human form of the Father's perfect image. There are three that bear witness in heaven—Father, Son, and Spirit—and these three are one. We do not see one competing over the other for greater notoriety; rather, we see unity and a perfect harmony between the Father, Son, and Spirit.

Whatever we dwell on and meditate on, whatever the god of our hearts is, will express itself in our lives. Renewing our minds is a spiritual matter that has everything to do with what we are

INNER IDENTITY AND HUMILITY

worshiping. If status and being notable is something being worshiped in your heart, if you dream and obsess for position in your church or workplace or group, then you will begin to build an altar in your heart toward that false god.

Jesus said a profound statement to Peter right after he cut the guard's ear off: "Put your sword in its place, for all who take the sword will perish by the sword" (Matthew 26:52). This statement is far more wide reaching than merely rebuking Peter for what he did that night. This statement has to do with whatever you choose to live by will consume you and eventually overtake you. If you choose to live by the spirit of Cain, you will build an altar to that false god. Eventually, the rocks you have stacked will collapse and implode all around your life.

The truth around this is that living your life for God is the only way not to be consumed and trampled by the spirit of Cain. Jesus said, "For whoever desires to save his life will lose it, but whoever loses his life for My sake will find it" (Matthew 16:25). Jesus is the only way to the Father; the spirit of Cain cannot get you to Him. If we truly want the blessing and acceptance of God, we must go through the blood of Jesus and the relationship He has provided for us through the cross.

Renewing our minds and changing the cultural tide looks like a people who have become so in love and obsessed with Jesus that they have seen the eyes of the Father and had the Holy Spirit whisper into their ears their own personal identity, purpose, and calling. It is in this moment that the achievements of others are no longer threats to our personal security; rather, they are beautiful scenery to look out upon and marvel at God's endless riches in Christ.

THE SPIRIT OF CAIN

Jesus is the way, the truth, and the life—no one comes to the Father except through Him (John 14:6). And it is in this truth that we find the answer to the spirit of Cain. When we realize that each man, woman, and child can be approved, accepted, and honored by God without a fraction being subtracted from another person, this iris will be destroyed, no longer able to envy and conspire, no longer driven with jealousy and hatred. Knowing the Lord intimately stops you from looking horizontally, like Cain and so many others have done throughout history. Rather, it causes us to look vertically, up into the eyes of our victorious King.

Understanding the psychology of these issues is fundamental to grasp if we are to fully understand the unaddressed, unhealed weaknesses in our emotional state that make a doorway for the spirit of Cain to operate in our lives. It is my hope that you would identify any "broken" areas in your heart as you read, and thus turn to the Lord for healing.

One of the greatest and most destabilizing flaws in a human being is insecurity. For the individual who does not know who they really are, it causes a desperation to emerge within that can have many faces or expressions. Insecurity can cause a developed superficial facade of boldness and confidence to appear as personality or character while all the while being tormented by emotions of not belonging, not being accepted by others, feeling inferior, and feeling threatened by those around us who are confident. Insecurity makes us feel as if we never belong.

Jealousy is prevalent in people who are insecure because an obsession arises that fixates on other people's perceived happiness, material possessions, the favor another carries, relationships,

INNER IDENTITY AND HUMILITY

status, or positions. There was an amazing moment for me, with the young man I mentioned in the previous chapter, when God warned me that he would act like Cain in our relationship. The competition in his heart did in fact cause many problems in my own life. There came a time in his life in which everything he thought he was building was apparently brought to a halt by God in His mercy so this man could reassess his life and move forward more whole.

I did my best to be with him and spend time with him when I could, because everyone needs to be shown mercy. I was doing my best to win a friend out of this person who had done nothing but compete with me. I took him out for a Coca-Cola and to play a few games of pool and share our hearts. As we played, I did my best to encourage him and counsel him. It was at that moment when everything that God had told me over a decade earlier was revealed as true.

He started by saying, "You know, Andrew, I've always been threatened and jealous of you. I've seen you as my biggest threat to get promoted in this church. I've always wanted to be like you—your confidence and personality, even the way you dress, has had me jealous. I've always looked up to you, but I haven't expressed that; instead, I've done everything to compete against you. And I'm sorry." Of course I forgave him and we carried on playing pool.

But then he continued, "I've had these constant mind games that have driven me—that's how I have dealt with my reality of feeling inferior. I created these alternate realities in my head in which I have relabeled people and circumstances in my life and seen people as markers to beat. I have had to be the best at everything—number one—and it's been an escapism of what's really going on inside." I was so glad he was finally recognizing this, finally getting it out; yet, at the same time, I was shocked hearing just how twisted and tormenting this had become for him.

People who are insecure have a fixation with people who have more than they do, or are successful in the areas they themselves desire to be successful in. This becomes a love-hate relationship for them psychologically, as, in the very same moment, they will love the prestige and hate the person for having it all. This is because, although it's what they wanted, it speaks of what they don't have and therefore devalues them and creates a message of being a failure, dictating huge personal insecurity. It's a confusing psychological state of mind, to say the least. This emotional trap will torment a person who does not know who they really are.

Competition is born from this breeding ground of insecurity. Competition from here becomes "the bulldozer effect" that squashes other people in the room who have potential. Both insecurity and jealousy can only exist due to the absence of one thing, and that is identity, which can only come from intimacy with Father God.

Remember, when friends or mentors affirm you, that is a complement. However, when God the Father affirms you, then you discover who you really are—you not only experience worth but you glimpse your own destiny and purpose, for your God-breathed identity has come. Insecurity inside of a person will often bring out some of the most hideous human behavior known to humanity. You can witness the most primal and base human

INNER IDENTITY AND HUMILITY

survival actions that will stop at nothing to defend itself against the threat that jealousy or a perceived need to compete against another person will bring. There may be no one more desperate than the individual who has little to no identity and who competes against others to find some form of imagined meaning. We must find freedom and healing as a people.

If people remain wounded in this area, the most socially aggressive and unstable elements that can be found in relationships will be present. I have been amazed at the amount of millionaires I have talked to who affirm this very thing. When I ask them what their driving force to succeed was, nine times out of ten they reply, "I used to have nothing. I am afraid that if I stop working I will go back to that again."

It is this same type of driving force that torments people with insecurity and jealousy. Their foundation and identity have not yet been grounded in Christ Jesus, and so they find the need to compare themselves with others, creating a downward spiral of insecure and jealous mentalities. They are driven by thoughts like, you do not have what that person has; you have not been promoted like that person has, even though you should have been—they don't deserve that. And, a person who is really honest with himself or herself, will acknowledge that his or her thoughts have become quite demented.

Insecure people will have scheming and physiologically twisted mind games constantly consuming their minds, causing thoughts to come about the person who has more than they do or has a promotion above them in a specific area of life. It's a mindset that sees everything and everyone in an imaginary hierarchal system with only one ladder up over the next person who stands in the way. This mind-set obstructs the joy of celebrating another's blessing or success and creates an everyman-out-for-himself attitude. It destroys the ability to trust, and it creates a purely self-centered focus.

A personal belief and philosophy of mine has always been that trust is the foundation required in any genuine relationship, whether it is romantic, family, church, or business. If trust is broken, then how can a stable team ever be formed? Trust and stability are the key ingredients to the longevity of any team. A group may be able to work together temporarily with a certain amount of success, even for a few years in some cases, but when the spirit of Cain lurks in the shadows of people's mind-sets with mistrust, jealousy, competition, and vengefulness, then it will only be a matter of time until this affects the whole team. This is, of course, unless it is healed or addressed.

How did you feel the last time one of your friends purchased a new car or home that was much nicer than yours? Did you feel immediately insufficient and insecure? Or were you still satisfied with your older model while being completely happy for their new gain? This is a good test as to where you are at in your life. This is not to condemn anyone, but rather to encourage us all to constantly be examining our hearts to ensure we are spiritually healthy.

Dwelling on and rehearsing these competitive and jealous mind-sets is nothing short of agreeing with demonic torment. The spirit of Cain looks for access into people's minds and then begins to convince the person that perceived insecurities and jealousies are actually a reality. Once this spirit has achieved this reality in the mind of an individual, the power of suggestion and

INNER IDENTITY AND HUMILITY

persuasion is easily achieved. And the individual, who is now in agreement with a demon spirit, will act more like a pawn, easily controlled, being tormented by competition and jealousy. And something like Cain and Abel will begin to unfold in his or her life.

Chapter 10

A KINGDOM WITH NO EVIL COMPETITION

With the direction and help of the Holy Spirit, my wife and I have watched and help build a culture in our Auckland, New Zealand, and our Orange County, California, churches. The culture looks like a people who love Jesus and walk with Father God, actually honoring each other for who they are uniquely in God. This culture looks like people celebrating, empowering, and supporting others as they grow and function in their individual gifts and callings at different levels of maturity and development. A culture of honor looks like an environment that desires personal and corporate growth while not allowing selfish ambition to bring on competition.

THE SPIRIT OF CAIN

But creating this type of culture has taken hard work. It is a complete counterculture to what is found in the world and, I'm sad to admit, also in many churches today. It is a constant task to maintain and facilitate this type of atmosphere. It's a nonthreatening state of culture in community in which everyone has equal opportunity to grow into their callings, gifts, and functions in different capacities. Ambition, jealousy, and competition must be neutralized and painted as a destructive attribute both individually and corporately; not just in the people but in the leaders also. What's on the head flows into the body, so freedom must begin with those who lead in corporate settings.

Some people have a gifting in hospitality and they have amazing functions in the church and community to operate in those ways. Gone are the days when the only spiritual function and calling in the church was the preacher in the pulpit on Sundays. That perception creates competition or a redundant stagnancy for many who would see that there is no hope for them to personally develop and grow into their calling.

Some churches see massive spiritual fruit coming out of their media teams; people in these ministry areas can touch the world by creating one video or film. Imagine making one short multimedia movie that goes viral and touches masses of people who then see and hear the hope of the cross. Those few hours spent in the media studio can reap untold harvests in heaven, which no one on earth will possibly ever see this side of heaven.

We have become creatures who are visual and results driven, which creates the competition that sets a man against his brother. However, God sees things differently. The only person who needs to be competed against on some level is your former self—are you

A KINGDOM WITH NO EVIL COMPETITION

progressing toward freedom and growth from who you were? The truth is that we should always be looking to increase and moving further into the blessing of God the Father for our own lives.

I have been so blessed seeing the growth of people and the culture in my church after seeing something quite the opposite in past experiences. When people truly fall in love with the Creator and King of heaven, competition loses its power in their hearts, and the affection and approval of the One is the only true desire that remains. When His affection that is set upon you is realized, the progress and accolades of another person do not move or threaten your identity or potential in any way. You are freely able to celebrate others, knowing that every person on the face of the earth has unlimited potential and destiny in Christ—and all this without taking away from another person. Envy is truly disempowered when authentic love is present.

After experiencing personally and corporately in church this unhealthy spirit of competition, I am so blessed to be a part of a community that warmly celebrates each person's role and function in the church body, as well as excited to see people progressively growing into maturity toward their call. Even from a lead pastor's point of view, growth in a congregation is not a threat to the lead role; it is the validation of the role. Momentary success without legacy is failure, and any leader desiring legacy must grasp this concept.

There is no competition in the kingdom of God, only honor and unity. In Psalm 110 David saw into the future, where Jesus was spoken to as an equal to God the Father and invited into the reward of His sacrifice by being told to sit at the Father's right

THE SPIRIT OF CAIN

hand until His enemies were made His footstool. The culture is so different in heaven than it is presently on earth. Earth, and all of its sin, has conditioned our minds to automatically calculate how to compete for the most material things, or how to be better than others, and this is even taking place inside the church.

When sin entered the world, Adam and Eve knew lack for the first time. In that moment they had to compensate for something that was apparently missing, as insecurity entered their hearts and began to define who they were. This was the first time that insecurity ever touched humanity on an enormous level, to the point that they needed to sow together fig leaves to make clothes to cover their nakedness. Humanity has not stopped being motivated by this lack and insecurity.

God's goal is to return us to the accepted state of sonship and daughterhood through the adoption made available at the cross. When a person receives a revelation of what Jesus has actually achieved and the worth of what it actually looks like to be grafted into the royal family of heaven, then that person begins to see that we each have our own unique and inalienable identity in Christ Jesus. Because of this we can truly begin to celebrate others instead of feeling threatened by them.

The ransom dictates your worth. Your worth was paid for with the blood of Jesus and by the death of the only Son of the God of the universe. Do we really understand the value of this? If we truly understood this value, we would be a whole lot more secure in our worth to God, and we would stop seeing ourselves as cheap and having no worth.

A kingdom with no competition looks like a world of harmony and life, a community that empowers others instead of

A KINGDOM WITH NO EVIL COMPETITION

speaking evil of them. A kingdom with no competition looks like a world that becomes incredibly efficient as each member of that kingdom comes into maximum productivity and potential as they are encouraged and empowered by their peers to grow into everything they personally have been called to be. Can you imagine a world like this? Can we change? I believe we can.

Humanity was designed by God to excel in the most amazing ways. But God never designed us to compete against each other to the measure of being in unhealthy competition with one another. In God's design, there is a world in which every person excels perfectly into their specialized gifts, and their immediate community makes room for the gift to be expressed. This shows value and worth to that individual, knowing that each person is an element of the greatest tapestry ever imagined—and that every person is needed. As each need, task, or opportunity comes up, requiring various specific gifts, the community of people honor and empower the person who is called to that area. Everyone understands their inner identity does not come from what they do but rather who they are as sons and daughters of God. Fallen human nature cannot take advantage of wrong motives and jealousy.

One of my favorite moments of how much God wants us to walk in honor and humility—not in competition—is when Jesus comes down to the river where John the Baptist is baptizing people. John had a legitimate ministry that was publicly recognized. Jesus could have approached that scene and demanded His status as God to prove and highlight the fact that He was more powerful than John, that He was the One who was to come. Instead of this, however, we see Jesus submit to John and ask to be baptized by him. As Jesus comes up out of the water, the Father affirms Jesus. The Spirit descends like a dove upon Him, then the Father's voice resounds from heaven: "This is My beloved Son, in whom I am well pleased" (Matthew 3:17). It is the perfect picture of identity and empowerment.

Then we see yet another and equally powerful aspect of a kingdom without competition. John the Baptist did not compete with Jesus; rather, he sent his followers to follow the Son of God. We do not read about John the Baptist being jealous of Jesus' following or His fame. John's ministry was almost thankless, and yet we do not see any resentment, jealousy, or competition toward Jesus. John showed Jesus the honor and empowerment that the Pharisees refused to give Him.

This is the model of the answer to the spirit of Cain. This is God demonstrating His kingdom that operates on the earth in unity. This is the same God who asked Cain where Abel was now setting the benchmark and path for the way we must all follow in our brotherly and sisterly relationships. And this is what the New Jerusalem will look like. Imagine an empire in which no one is hated for what they have but honored and empowered for what they are, a place where jealousy is nonexistent and no person will resent his or her brother or sister.

God wants us to cleanse our hearts and be transformed and renewed in the thinking of our minds so that we can build Him purity of unity in our churches, communities, and relationships. Unity commands the blessing, and the enemy knows this and has warred against humanity ever since the beginning of time. We, the empowered sons and daughters of God, are now commissioned to take authority given to us by God to rule, have

A KINGDOM WITH NO EVIL COMPETITION

dominion, and multiply, not just in number but in unity, within the gospel of peace. Recognizing and honoring the diversity in others brings greater strength to the group and is a big step toward genuine unity.

Allow this dream of God to be planted in your heart and spirit. Begin to build this dream of His world into your own personal life, then out into your community—you are responsible to be this, to live this, and to demonstrate this, no matter how others around you behave. Imagine for a moment, a local church or even the body of Christ as a whole, that doesn't compete against itself. Do we truly realize how much more progress we would be making regarding the Great Commission if we spent our time reaching the lost rather than turning brother against brother?

Just like our physical body cannot compete against itself, neither can the body of Christ compete with each other. The only time we see the physical body competing against itself is in the case of cancer. When we as the body of Christ learn to stop devouring each other, then we will be a truly glorious bride that advances from glory to glory, living in breakthrough and victory, ready for the Bridegroom's return.

If we are no longer to compete and oppose each other, then what are we to do? The opposite of competing against one another is honoring and empowering each other in our God-given identity and destiny. Jesus presented a selfless gospel, not a message of self-promoting or selfish ambition for everyone to follow. Then He said to them all, "If anyone desires to come after Me, let him deny himself, and take up his cross daily, and follow me" (Luke 9:23). Jesus clearly led by example in the path He demonstrated. Denying yourself also includes preferring others over and above yourself.

The spirit of competition robs the body of Christ of her true strength and beauty. We are called to be a people who are encouraging, building up and preferring others' gifts and anointing, and in doing so pushing the called ones forward in their gifts and ministries. If the Holy Spirit had to wait forty days until the level of unity had been reached and there was a oneness for Him to descend and inhabit the early church in the upper room in Jerusalem, then where have we gone wrong thinking that He will not be grieved and withdraw when we are behaving in anything but unity? Unity draws the blessing of God.

If you are a pastor, I would challenge you to call another pastor in your city that you don't usually connect with and take them out to lunch and begin to build a real relationship with him. Focus on their strengths, find common ground in your conversation, and encourage them with no agenda but unity and godly love. If there has been any competitive nature in your relationship with that other pastor, respond out of your spirit man, not your carnal nature, and go the opposite route. Be a bridge of honor; walk in humility, encouragement, and empowerment rather than competition and rivalry. Find out what you can do to be a blessing to him. And then watch a spiritual blessing come on your life, ministry, and church as a result.

The same solution is true for any facet or form of relationship. Honor goes a long way and can open all kinds of doors of favor for your life. Don't attack people because of your jealousy or envy, and don't look for reasons to discredit them. Discipline your mind to not even entertain hostile thoughts toward them

A KINGDOM WITH NO EVIL COMPETITION

of any jealous, competitive, or hateful nature. Rather, take those types of thoughts captive and reject them from growing in your mind. Encourage and honor these people's strengths. Can you imagine what would happen if all the pastors in a city did this? We need to understand that there are different theologies and denominations out there, but there is still only one bride. What would revival really look like if churches in a city came together recognizing that each one has a role to play?

There have been a few times, in my church in southern California, I partnered with churches from a completely different denomination to reach out to the community. Many pastors and church leaders may shake their heads at this, because they would begin to ask themselves, what if my people go to that church instead of mine? Or, if people are saved, which church will they go to? These thoughts are nothing but unhealthy competition. We are one body, one baptism, one gospel, one bride, and one God.

If preachers, friends, family, churches, congregations, worship teams, and church departments would show honor instead of this evil competition, we would see genuine revival rather than bursts of God's presence that get sabotaged by pride and ego and all kinds of selfish ambition. There is only one kingdom in heaven—there won't be different churches in heaven—and we will all be a part of one glorious family. Are you busy building your own kingdom? Are you actually connected with heaven? There are no schisms in God's world, no sects.

The same goes for personal and nonministry relationships too. If you are a person who has been in jealousy and rivalry with others, look how to serve that person or people with a genuine

THE SPIRIT OF CAIN

heart. Maybe it's time to look to build unity and not rivalry. Take accountability for your jealousy and envy issue, repent, and change your thinking. Allow this moment to be a pivotal marker of change in your life concerning this. Unity agrees with heaven, whereas rivalry agrees with the enemy. It's time we see this for what it is.

Now imagine the business world and your colleagues, cities, countries, and even all the ethnic groups operating in this honor rather than the spirit of Cain. My company recently carried out a project for a gentleman whom I discovered once the contract was underway was a top executive of one of the largest retail chain stores in the world. He took me into his office and began to tell me how impressed he was with the way I ran my company. Then he began to tell me who he was and what company he ran. Needless to say, I was honored to receive a complement from such a successful man. Recognizing just how much success he had experienced and achieved, I showed him incredible honor and offered to take him out to the nicest restaurant in the area so I could ask him questions about his success and learn from him. I wanted to search for pearls that could change my life! If more people showed honor to successful and anointed individuals instead of disdaining them, competing against them, and being consumed by jealousy, then success would be far more attainable for many more folks.

You see, honor is the opposite of jealousy and envy. If we can individually and as a generation authentically learn to celebrate and cheer the successes of others, our lives would begin to look incredibly different. We will be at peace with each other instead of tormented and consumed with rivalry. Wars would

A KINGDOM WITH NO EVIL COMPETITION

cease, companies would prosper and flourish, productivity would soar, and the world would be a little closer to Eden than we currently are!

Honoring a successful person will draw their favor toward you, possibly even engaging a conversation or relationship that ends up changing your life. Jealousy and envy of the success or position that someone has is actually far more discernible than you think. If you think you are doing a good job of hiding your disdain or rivalry toward another person, you most likely are not—it is far more obvious than it may appear.

Jealousy is extremely dishonoring. When jealously is expressed, a person always feels dishonor in the heart even if no words are exchanged. Dishonor repels people, as an insult will never draw out a warm smile. Jealously only robs you from the relationships God may want you to have. There is so much joy in genuinely honoring others, empowering their moment, role, success, or call.

Competition steals the joy of celebrating a brother or sister's promotion in the kingdom or workplace. Spiritual aristocracy does not exist in the true kingdom of heaven—there is no better or lesser person, gifts or not! Competition cuts a person down by devaluing them and causing them to feel like "the highest score" that has to be beaten. Make it the goal of your life in the area of relationships to counter this and show honor.

Rather than a culture of the strongest survive, it would be good if we supported those in leadership, authority, and service, those who receive more favor or blessings than us. The truth is that leading and being in a position of authority is often one of the more thankless and difficult roles in the world. For instance,

THE SPIRIT OF CAIN

being a pastor is an extremely difficult job—I would say in many cases more taxing and intense than running a business. However, to the ambitious and zealous young Christian who has a desire to rise and be brought into their call, there can most often be a misconception that pastoring is a great deal more glamorous than it really is. If people honestly knew the weighty responsibility and even burden that leading or pastoring can be at times, they would be a lot slower to compete or be jealous of these roles.

Insecure people or people who are still growing in identity and maturity can have an overly unhealthy desire for spiritual authority and power. This is not bad in and of itself, but if there is a lust for power and an attitude of entitlement, then this can lead to the same power struggle and enmity that Cain had with Abel—all rooted in self-seeking, jealousy, and envy.

Having read through this book, I pray that the trappings and strategies of this spirit would be apparent and a lot clearer to you so that you can be aware of the enemy's scheme against your life and so that you can be equipped to stand against the enemy's plans and defend your God-given inheritance and blessings. Honoring others who are honored by God is only achievable once we recognize that every single person has the unlimited capacity to excel and soar into the approval and blessing of God in a way that has nothing to do with the measure that has been shown to others.

God has not given away all He has, like it was when Isaac released his inheritance blessing to Jacob, and Esau was no longer eligible for the blessing. God, when honoring another person, is never out of resources in His heart to show honor to His sons and daughters who do right before Him. His ability to honor has

A KINGDOM WITH NO EVIL COMPETITION

a limitless abundance. The apostle Paul said in 2 Corinthians 10:12, "But they, measuring themselves by themselves, and comparing themselves among themselves, are not wise." It is God's desire that we look to Him and not anyone else to measure where we are and who we are.

Allow your heart to learn this and no longer look to your neighbor to benchmark your worth or acceptance. If you don't grasp this, then you will continue to buy into the same sin that crouched at Cain's door, which eventually expressed itself against Abel. The only person we can allow ourselves to look to for honor, inheritance, affirmation, and acceptance is the Lord God Almighty, Abba Father, the One who loves us all with no partiality. He is the One who defines who we are, causing us to rest secure in Him. It is in Him that we are set free from this spirit of unhealthy competition. It is only by the blood of Jesus and His suffering on the cross that we are set free from the spirit of Cain, choosing honor over competition.

Behold, how good and how pleasant it is

For brethren to dwell together in unity!

It is like the precious oil upon the head,

Running down on the beard,

The beard of Aaron,

Running down on the edge of his garments.

It is like the dew of Hermon,

Descending upon the mountains of Zion;

For there the Lord commanded the blessing—

Life forevermore.

Psalm 133:1–3

www.AndrewBillings.org